Aspects of Life

Aspects of Life

An Invitation to Think

Rajendra Swaroop Bhatnagar

PARTRIDGE
A Penguin Random House Company

To order additional copies of this book, contact
Partridge India
000 800 10062 62
orders.india@partridgepublishing.com

www.partridgepublishing.com/india

Contents

Contents

Pre-text

Most of us have experienced certain dichotomous aspects of life sometimes or other. Somehow we resolve or have resolved these dilemmas in given situation rationalizing to ourselves that we have done what we should have done. We are placed in a network of a great totality – we call universe. How to understand this relationship for in some way it affects all my thoughts and action. One of the puzzling questions arises from the fact of my attempt to understand nature. This attempt itself creates a rupture between me and nature. In other words 'I' as the one trying to understand and 'nature' there to be understood obviously get into an opposed position. A similar puzzle arises when we reflect on the relation between our minds (as separate from brain) with the body as considered material. Questions of free volition also arise from the same kind of duality. Are these dualities inevitable? These and related questions about suffering, our finitude, death and our relation with family, and society, press on your attention if you at all bother about your existence. These are not merely theoretical exercises but are intimately connected with one's outlook and life.

For me, having completed eight decades of my life, it was time to go through the thoughts relating to those conflicting situations and related issues in a more serene mood. What I learnt from my readings, what I heard from the wise men and women, and from my living experience, have gone into the articulation of the thoughts that I present in the following text.

Most of the things that I write are neither novel nor exhaustive. I have tried not to be pedantic and readers would not find quotes after quotes in the text except some interesting quotes given in the beginning of each essay. These are ideas which I would have liked to share with someone who could be patient enough to hear me. I would have loved to learn where my thoughts get derailed, or were irrelevant or unsound from my interlocutor.

Fortunately my friends Professor R.P. Garg, who had taught English Literature)now retired), and Shri Guru Chopra, who had worked for some corporate establishment in Mexico, USA and other places, were kind enough to go through some or whole of the text. Shri Garg saved me for several infelicitous expressions. Shri Chopra offered some constructive suggestions. Some of the essays were read by my Late daughter – Dr. Kaninika Bhatnagar, who was an Assistant Professor in the School of Technology, in Eastern Illinois University. She drew my attention to the complexities of issues I dealt with. My granddaughter, Panchhi, has helped me by setting the text in a unified way.

I hope my readers to share their critical thoughts with me to help in my thinking.

Rajendra Swaroop Bhatnagar,
Retd. Prof. of Philosophy, Rajasthan University,
Jaipur, India.
Email – brajen5@gmail.com

Humans and Nature

"A human being is a part of the whole called by us universe, a part limited in time and space. He experiences himself, his thoughts and feeling as something separate from the rest, a kind of optical delusion of his consciousness. This delusion is a kind of prison for us restricting us to our personal desires and to affection for a few persons nearest to us. Our task must be to free ourselves from the prison by widening our circle of compassion to embrace all living creatures and the whole of nature in its beauty." Albert Einstein.

Anyone who ventures into a study of *Vaidik samhitas*, cannot remain unstruck by the close and intimate relationship between the *rsi* and the *devata* (who held some one or the other natural force in her or his control and regulation- in fact the natural force was not merely a power with which the *devata* was endowed but the two were even identified). The *rsi* prepares for fire (let us remember that those were not the days when you had a lighter or matchstick to light something instantly, one had to spend good time and force rubbing pieces of wood or stone to get a spark and thereby a flame), prepares *soma* juice for the *devata*, which was supposed to induce energy and strength, and then he would sing praises to coax the *devata* to come and enjoy the *soma*. Having propitiated, the *rsi* would request the *devata* for good harvest, offspring, health, knowledge and well-being. The *rsi* felt that he had an obligation towards the *devata* and he believed that if he fulfils his obligation, the *devata* in turn would take care of his well-being. Such was the relationship which the *vaidika rsies* had with Indra, Varuna, Mitra,Usa, Savitri, Aryama, Visnu, Agni et cetera.

We learn that people of ancient times would worship trees, rivers even some of the animals such as snakes (who probably saved the fields from the rats). It is said in the *Gita* (3.12), that if someone consumes what gods bestow without making her or his offerings, then such a person is a thief. In order to understand the message of these sayings, we should think of nature and natural forces in place of god or gods. The relation between life and the elements – five *mahabhutas* as known in the Indian tradition, is very intimate, as would be obvious to anyone who takes the trouble to think about the matter. The Sun and its light and heat, the air which allows us to breath, the water which quenches our thirst, the soil which stores all that we get in the form of cereals, vegetables, fruits and so on, the space or *akasa* which permits us to move about, clearly show that life would be impossible without them. The story of *sagar-manthan* (churning the ocean) is a classic example of what treasures can nature bestow if right intention, proper skill, courage and hard labour are put in.

The scientists tell us that the conditions conducive and supportive of life in its immense bio-diversity as found on earth, are not found on other planets so far known. In fact earth is like mother. If she did not suckle us we would not exist. But nature has not always been treated as benign and homely. It has another face also. There are places on earth where either sand or rocks abound and where there is no water. There are places where temperature is either very high or very low. There is land where the soil does not bestow its gifts to nourish us. Living in conditions like these, is to struggle hard for survival. Then there are natural calamities. There are floods. There are tornadoes and cyclones. There are earthquakes or volcanic eruptions. Obviously in these conditions nature does not show its kind and benign visage. It is fierce, cruel and devastating. One has to fight with it. One has to win it over. Or bow down against it or learn the ways which permit survival.

Sometime human beings have felt that natural calamities are the ways in which divine anger becomes manifest. Nature is angry because we have stopped living rightly. We have become greedy, cruel and sinful. Readers would remember the controversy between Gandhi and Tagore, when Gandhi expressed the view that Bihar earth quake in 1936 was a divine punishment for our sin of untouchability. Besides, in *Mahabharat,* we are told that if the king does not perform his duties properly and there is disorder in his kingdom then some calamity or the other afflicts his kingdom. On the contrary, if everything is in order and the king performs his duties properly, nature remains bountiful. Thus there seems to have been a belief in the intimate relation between the order of nature and the order of society or polity. Human beings and their doings are closely related with the nature and its workings.

Tagore as is well known had a great reverence for nature as well as for the cosmic order. Yet he thought it to be odd and foolish to see any relationship between the natural happenings and the doings of men. The two realms are independent. But there is another context in which the relation between the doings of men and the natural happenings do seem to have a close relationship. Almost daily we read in the news papers that our style of consumption, limitless exploitation of natural resources, emission of harmful gasses resulting from the use of certain technical gadgets and deforestation are adding to the global warming and damaging the ozone layer which protects us from the harmful rays of Sun. Though most people recognize that human doings are disturbing and damaging the ecological balance yet in practice people do not seem to care much about what is happening or conscious of their style of living.

In fact while we think about something we unconsciously draw a line between ourselves and the object about which we are thinking. When we reflect on nature, we tend to think that nature is there and we are here. That is, there is a radical distinction between us and nature. The fact is that we are not conscious of the fact that we are there at all. We are all the time occupied with the objects we think about. Thus it does not occur to us that we ourselves form an integral component of nature. If we realized that we are ourselves part of nature, then it is obvious, that we would also realize that our doings are in a way part of natural happenings. Consequently there must be some kind of causal relation between the various chains of natural happenings including the doings of ours, that is, we human beings.

That we human beings form part of nature is patent from the very fact that several disciplines are engaged in understanding human beings from several points of view. Psychology, anthropology, medicine, sociology, politics, history, literature and philosophy are all devoted to understand human beings both as individuals as well as in their collectivities in terms of their doings – good or bad, constructive or destructive, and also in terms of what they have thought, discovered and invented. Human beings attempt to understand human beings. This is inevitable for it is crucial for their interaction. The process of understanding goes on informally and formally, deliberately and unconsciously. The peculiarity of self involvement marks these disciplines out from several others where no subjectivity seems to be involved in the study of the object such as, natural sciences..

Natural sciences are said to be concerned with the various aspects of nature and natural objects in a way in which their investigations are carried on without any involvement of the subjective element. In fact, one of the requirements of scientific attitude and study is to brush aside the subjective element totally. However, lately scientists have realized that it is not possible to keep the scientist as observer completely out of the scientific picture. Yet, epistemologically speaking, it is clear that observation requires the acceptance of the duality of subject and object – what is being observed and the observer. This duality in some sense keeps the subject out of the picture. As noticed above, this draws a line between humans and nature which is a useful fiction like the line of equator on a map.

It seems that we are fated to undulate between subjecthood and objecthood. From another point of view what happens in natural events and what happens within our subjective experiences also reveal some sort of affinity between humans and nature. Writers describing human emotions and feelings often fall back on certain characteristics of the natural happenings. Such a synchrony is also exploited by the dramatists and film makers. Literary metaphors also feed on such a relationship. Sun and light or life; dawn and hope; night and darkness, fall and dusk or evening; anger and fire; peace or gravity or seriousness and ocean; determination and rock or mountain; organism or organization and tree; bravery and lion; cunningness and fox and so on indicate how the happenings within the experiential aspect of life and happening in the diurnal routine of nature and its constituents are seen to reflect each other.

The *rsi* in the *Rg Veda* wonders how the Sun nourishes truth and destroys falsehood – *rtam pipartyanrtam ni tarit* (1.152.3). Look at some expressions from a recent text – "The desert-wandering Hebrew prophet was conscious of God in the wind that rattled through dry vegetation and penetrated his very bones,...(180)"; "A block of seagulls will scatter as a child runs toward them, and then they will invariably reassemble a few dozen yards up the beach. When not excited into action by the mechanism of choice, a quantum system tends naturally toward its least excited or zero-point energy state.(211)"; "Let them (stray thoughts) come, observe them as you might observe a twig carried by a river and let them pass away. Don't fight them, because to fight them is to dam the river.(210)" – All these quotes are from *Code Name God*, by Mani Bhaumik, Penguin, 2005.

Notice how the wind in the desert, block of seagull, twig and river help the author to express some abstruse ideas for these natural aspects which are open to external perceptual experience seem so close to what goes on in the mind which remains opaque to observation and which can only be felt or experienced in a subjective way. Any number of examples can be cited from the creative works telling the same story.

As is said, the *'pind'* (the atom) reveals the *'brahmanda'* (the cosmos). Obviously, the simile cannot be stretched too far. Natural happenings reveal an order and system which is sometime interpreted as a design of some cosmic power. It is because of the regularities involved in such an order and the system that it is possible to investigate the laws underlying them. While what goes on in the mind is often understood in terms of some natural event or object, it does not reveal an order or system in the same regular way. The understanding of human beings as rational beings often becomes a doubtful proposition. Perhaps when it is said that the atom reveals the cosmos (an orderly entity), comparison is based only in certain select respects.

There is a deeper cleavage between the human nature and the nature with capital N. I am not sure if such a distinction can be maintained with any great certainty for our understanding of the cosmic nature is only nascent. Yet it does help to understand an important aspect of human nature. Human nature is infected by a duality involved in self reflection which does not seem to be obvious in the case of cosmic nature. Freud believed that it is not a duality which distinguishes the psychic structure but a triune composition which came to be known as Super-ego, Ego and Id. The Id represented the motivational forces which were supposed to be largely unconscious and instinctual, Ego indicated the conscious level where one was conscious of one's identity as an 'I', and Super-ego stood for some sort of conscience which would distinguish between right and wrong and which represented the social control.

Ego remains in a constant tension because of the different kind of commands it receives from the other two forces. One may agree with the psychoanalytical view of psychic structure or not, it is clear that most desires which propel human beings into action seem to be blind to rules and limits. It is also a fact that an individual living amongst other individuals cannot do whatever one likes, ignoring completely the presence of and relations with the other individuals. Thus an individual is supposed to observe restraints in what one wants to obtain, to do, and consume. There is a moving force and there is an awareness of limit or rule and one has to resolve the tension between the two.

Obviously such a situation involves self-reflection. One reflects on what one does, did, or plans to do. Most of the time our reflection consists of thinking why there was a miscarriage in a certain plan and what can be done again avoiding the pitfalls ignored earlier. One also reflects on what goes on in the mind and on one's situation. Occasionally one reflects on the sheer fact of one's existence. Why at all I exist. What is my place in the existence in the wider perspective? Does my life have any meaning beyond meeting the contingencies of day to day living? A very important feature of self-reflection is that it is self-corrective though unfortunately not effective to the same extent..

This self-corrective feature, as is evident from above, is either pragmatic or has a wider and deeper import. Failures and miscarriages compel the agent to think about the whole affair as to where things have gone wrong. That the very ends of the project were wrong or unworthy is not the issue which causes worry to the agent. S/he is concerned basically about the process or procedure rather than the end. S/he resolves to see that the mistakes or the neglects are not repeated and proceeds in the venture again. The ends are pragmatic and the rationality is instrumental. It is obvious that this observation applies to all kinds of projects – good or bad.

The deeper form of self-corrective measure has to do with the transformational orientation of being. Such a measure would presuppose a proper understanding of the distant goal or meaning of life. This in turn would require a world view and one's place in it. Such a view transcends the survival necessities. Consideration of utility is no more dominant. A reflection on one's beliefs and doings from such a perspective, and an attempt to examine and modify them would form the content and process of the deeper self-correction. If there is cooperation, harmony, amity, fellow feeling, or feeling of being at home with oneself and the others, one can assure oneself that self-reflective and self-corrective processes are at work

These processes direct our attention to the nature of humans themselves. This is obvious that human beings are in some respects different and distinguished from other living beings. The mass and structure of brain, physiognomic features, the structure of larynx and tongue, the structure of hands, possibility of erect posture are physical features which separate human beings from other living beings. Though at the rudimentary level their cognitive capabilities are common with the other beings, at a higher level they definitely mark them out. Highly developed rational capacity, their imaginative reach, the capacity of controlled emotional deportment and their ability to use language, the ability to create artifacts of all kinds and establish institutions are characteristics which distinguish them from all other living beings. These are features about which there is no doubt or debate.

Problems arise when attempts are made to determine the human nature on the basis of what they do. They do good things and they do bad things. We hear of Mahavir, Buddha, Jesus, Mohammad, Panna Dai, numerous saints and sufies, Gandhi, Vinoba Bhave, Mother Teresa and many others who dedicated their lives for the good and well being of mankind. On the other hand there have been cruel and vain people like Chingez Khan, Stalin, Hitler and many others whose dastardly acts, it is difficult to forget. Apart from these great and notorious names, acts of cruelty, deceit and destruction on the one hand and acts of sacrifice, selfless service, and love can be read off from the news paper any morning.

In the majority of cases same people will be found to be doing good and sometime doing what is wrong and sinful. But in cases of some people it is found they frequently do things which are either undesirable or praiseworthy. Perhaps no body would have bothered about human nature if everyone were good, did her or his duties, and loved others. One is compelled to think about human nature mostly when it is found that someone habitually goes on acting destructively and violently. Not only with regard to some particularly devilish people, but anyone might wonder about oneself, when evil thoughts take hold of one's mind. The question simply is why someone acts violently or deceitfully? This may be found in the case of anyone.

Is the root of evil to be found in the essence of human nature itself, or the circumstances in which a certain individual is placed, or in some other hidden source? It is well known that some children were rescued from non-human habitat such as wild woods and who behaved just like the wild animals and who could not use normal language. These exceptional cases point to the importance of human beings living amongst human beings. Human beings are human beings because they have an opportunity to live amongst their kind. There is another aspect which needs attention and that has to do with the process of growth and maturation of a human being. Everyone is aware of the fact that sometime some individuals do not attain proper growth and maturation. They suffer from some biological defect or the other. However, human compassion and care are found to help such unfortunate individuals.

It would be perhaps not right to think of deliberately evil acts in respect of either wolf-child or the underdeveloped child. On the other hand the possibility of some disturbing gene cannot altogether be denied. In any case, it is also an important fact, that genetic make-up undergoes modification by the environment. Thus the source of evil disposition may not be found wholly in the human nature from the genetic point of view. It may be defective bringing up, some traumatic experience, difficulties one faces in day to day living because of the privative conditions existing in the society, hurts, insults, and humiliations one may have had to suffer on some or other account or some such cause which may lead to an unhealthy attitude and disposition.

The most interesting and instructive fact of human nature is the ability of human beings to recognize their error, mistake or wrong and their determination to rectify the slips and to move on the right path. This of course, involves the understanding of what is wrong and what is right. Human beings are capable to undertake such an enquiry. This is what makes them rational and what distinguishes them from the other living beings. One may ask that if such is the case, why not the people, who are blind to the sufferings they are causing to others and who wade in their own interests and pleasure, are able to see that they are pursuing a wrong path? We have already noticed some of the causes responsible for such an indifferent attitude. Besides, there are individual differences and in case of each individual the description and explanation of deviation from social concerns are likely to be different. The possibility of change of attitude and style of life remains open.

It is a commonplace that an individual at some particular moment should be seen as a product of organism and environment nature and nurture. The organism should be understood not merely as a biological system but must be seen as including personal and social aspects also, and similarly environment must be understood as including the social and cultural features also. These features introduce immense variety. Thus each individual is likely to reveal features different from the other. This prevents us to formulate any generalized principle in relation to human nature. In fact, according to one view, there is no human nature. Humans do not have nature, they have a history. At a given moment, of definition of an individual can only be described by what he does or how he acts. Dramatic changes occur in the history of individuals. Sometime the transformations are beyond comprehension. Sinners are known to have become saints and saints are known to have become sinners. Philosophers have increasingly found the discourse of essences as slippery. According to one trend in Buddhism anything that exists has no essential property. For everything depends for its definition on something else. Thus there are no essences.

There is another view in Indian thinking according to which most of the troubles that one faces in the world are due to the fact that one wanders away from one's real nature or has forgotten one's true nature. The true nature of a human being, according to this view, is to be found in one's pure subjectivity. So long as an individual identifies oneself with one's body or bodily features, one fails to realize one's true nature. The true nature indwells in spirit, soul or atma. *Atma* is conceived as pure consciousness and beyond feelings and desires. Thus it is identified with pure bliss or happiness. The problem with this transcendental view is that it ultimately leads to complete withdrawal from action and thereby from the world in which one lives.

This view though claims itself to be descriptive in the sense that it claims to describe and convey as to what reality is, it seems to work as a prescriptive measure for it summons the individual to move in a different direction and work for one's emancipation or liberation. As a conclusion this view follows from an analysis of human situation seen as full of misery and sorrow. The locus of suffering and sorrow is body. Desires and cravings are situated within the bodily requirements. When the desires remain unfulfilled, or not completely fulfilled, or are frustrated for one reason or the other, one feels pain, despair, and depression. Sometime one is simply enraged in not succeeding and the rage takes away one's reason and control and one is driven to violence and destructive acts. Thus the body turns out to be a culprit and a source for all the misery.

Such a view prevents us from noticing that it is because of the body that one can perceive all that is good and beautiful in the world, that it is because of the body that one can act and perform one's duty and good deeds. In fact, the content and direction of good deed is often seen as doing good for someone else. Such deeds can be described as making the lives of other people comfortable. Bringing up a child, serving an old person, tending a sick person, cooperating with the other person in some desirable venture where one needs help, and so on will not be possible if we do not accept the bodily existence of other people and ourselves.

The joy or delight one attains in listening to music, in watching a good painting, sculpture or a monument, in reading poetry or fiction, or watching children play and be happy, or doing some constructive or creative work, or just in being engrossed in doing something worthwhile – are possible because one is endowed with limbs to work with, senses to cognize and feel or in other words because one is equipped with a body.

Sometime the argument is advanced that the pursuit of pleasure in the world ultimate results in its opposite. So it is better not to indulge in it at all. That can be done only when one becomes oblivious of one's body. This is true only if one indulges in pleasure seeking with no limits or control and without concern for the other persons and even at the cost of exploiting or demeaning them. But this would result into an absurdity if the argument proceeds ignoring the simple, harmless even invigorating small pleasures of life.

It is odd and impractical to anchor the true nature of human beings in a transcendental existence completely dissociated with the living and real concerns of the life. Most human beings, largely in their day to day activities neither indulge in their cravings limitlessly nor conspire to harm others unnecessarily. Limitless indulgence, conspiracies, exploitation are really practiced by the few whose hunger for power and pelf does not know any end. The large majority of people on the globe struggle for the minimum needs of life to be met. It appears to me that the transcendental message is really meant for the few affluent individuals who seem to consider the world and its resources as meant only for their enjoyment.

Yet I would prize the moments when seemingly all projects come to cease, no desire bothers, everything seems to be fine with the world, I have no grievance against myself, I seem to be completely at peace with myself. Nature is no more other or alien. No bridge is needed between two of us.

We have noticed the various usages of the term 'nature' – it applies to any thing that may exist and also to the entirety of things irrespective of time frame. Specifically, our profound concerns have to do with the nature of human beings on the one hand, and the nature of which we are parts, which surrounds us and comprehends us. We also found how close the two are, sometime forming the inner and external of existence. We talk about them in descriptive, prescriptive and also normative sense. If only each one of us could perceive the intimate relation between us and the nature around, and limit the consumption within reasonable bounds, found time to be with nature and its wonders at some moments and be grateful for all that we are provided by nature, life can be richer and full of happiness.

Mind and Matter

"What then am I? A thing that thinks. What is that? A thing that doubts,understands, affirms, denies, is willing, is unwilling, and also imagines and has sensory perceptions." Rene Descartes.

"If we approach homo sapiens from the perspective of natural history and the physical sciences, we can tell a coherent story of the constitution, development and behavioural capacities which encompasses particle physics, atomic and molecular theory, biology, physiology and materialistic neuroscience.' P.M.Churchland.

Mind is peculiar in the sense that it is open to inspection of the individual to whom it belongs and to no other. Scientists can rip open the brain, use various techniques to understand its anatomy and physiology, but in an essential aspect they are not able to move further. What a scientist may feel about her or his own mind, s/he is not able to find any physical correlate in the brain which may be experienced in the same way. Since some scientists find that the notion of mind and consciousness do not help much in the investigation of brain and its functions, they find it convenient to push them aside.

However, there is a way in which some sort of relation between mind and brain may be studied. The results of stimulation of parts of brain and the changes occurring in the other parts of the body as well as the verbal report of the subject can be mutually related. The verbal reports might refer back to the feelings or experiential aspect which the subject undergoes. The problem arises from the fact that the various terms used in respect of the mental functions such as thinking, willing, imagining, remembering, feeling, planning and so on do not have any identifiable locations in the body if they are taken to have their origin in some faculties other than the parts of brain. Yet it has become possible to identify parts in the brain which seem to be responsible for some of these functions. But the matching is still far from being very exact.

This has led thinkers to debate the issue of the relationship between mind and brain on the one hand, and mind and the body on the other. One source of the debate can be traced to the ontological dualism between mind and matter. Historically the roots of dualism lie both in the ancient Greek thought as well as in the Upanisadic thinking in India. In Upanisads they made a distinction between transcendental cum immortal self and the body, while Plato considered body as the tomb of the soul and Aristotle distinguished between separable reason and the body. If we wish to look at the problem from the point of view of the Indian thinkers, the problem becomes more complicated because of the linguistic disparities. What is understood as mind in the Western tradition and what is considered to be *'antah karana'* or *'buddhi'* in the Indian thinking are very different concepts. And yet there are several occasions when the Hindi *'manas'* is used as a translation of mind. The matter becomes more confused when we find that in Indian terminology the term *'hrdaya'* is also interchanged with *'mana'* or *'manasa'*.

In the day to day usage, the term *'mana'* is used as something which determines most of our thinking and activities. In fact the term is so rich in its usage that it comprehends multifarious aspects of mental life. It is closer in its usage to the other term *'hrdaya'*. In the sense of mind it is used as *'manasa'*. *Mana* as distinguished from *manas* seems to be closer to willing, in the sense of moving men to act in certain ways. Sometime it is used in the sense of attending or not attending something. It is also used for expressing negative or positive feeling. Thus *mana* and *manas* together will cover all those activities and aspects which have to do with mind. And as is well known mind is also used in as many ways as the terms *mana* and *manas* together. Descartes, the French philosopher, used the terms 'mind' or 'consciousness' in the sense of all the various mental functions. It is also the case, that *mana* is used as distinguished from *buddhi* and *ahamkara*. Sometime *mana* is used as a controlling or synthesizing function relating to senses and *buddhi*. All these considerations show that it is necessary to say beforehand how and in what sense one is using any of these terms.

In contrast to senses *mana, buddhi* and *ahamkara* are collectively called *antah karana*. Senses are directed towards external world and in their physical form can be observed

by others also. That however is not the case in respect of
antah karana, and it is for that very reason,that it is called
internal. The unusual thing about the *antah karan* is that it
is distinguished from pure consciousness. In the Samkhya
system, as noted elsewhere, *antah karana* and *cetana* or *citi*
are said to be radically different. *Antah karan* belongs to
prakrti which is said to be *jada* or inert or lifeless, while
cetana is conceived as *purusa.* In order to maintain the
possibility of experience and the activities, Samkhya also
teaches that both have their role in the empirical world or
samsara.. Without some kind of contact between the *purusa*
and *prakrti* human experience and activities would not be
possible. Unfortunately the theory of the contact remains as
problematic as the theory of interaction between mind and
body as postulated by Rene Descartes.

Since the two are defined or understood as radically
different from each other, neither the idea of contact nor the
idea of interaction is much helpful. This duality manifests
in another context also. Aristotle talked of separable reason
(a synonym for mind), and soul (the conscious principle or
entity) as distinct from the body and as beyond destruction
in contrast to the body which is destructible. However, there
is a little complication, so far as Indian beliefs are concerned.
Besides, pure consciousness and body, a third entity is
accepted which is called *suksma sarira* or *ling sarira* which
is in fact not a part of the body but an indication of the
lived experience of the *jiva* or the individual. *Suksma sarira*
is supposed to be the link between the two successive lives.
When an individual dies, the body decays and is consigned
to flames. *Atma* remains untouched with the *mahabhutas* or

the five elements. *Suksma sarira* which is neither body nor pure consciousness survives and gets housed in another body according to the deeds the individual had done in her earlier life. There is no concept comparable in the Western tradition which could be parallel to the notion of suksma sarir.

Much more can be found about the usage of these terms, but it seems that there has been an ambivalent attitude towards the relationship between mind and body, body as being treated as material in contrast to mind or soul which is treated as spiritual. There is much that is built up on the foundation of the distinction between mind and matter. In one context, whatever is material is associated with sensualism and consumerism, and is taken to be responsible for all that is lower in the hierarchy of values, and all the ills that afflict the human beings. On the contrary, the spiritual is supposed to raise the individual to a higher level, enable her or him to assess the worldly objects properly, emancipate her or him from the treacherous traps of worldly attractions, and allows her or him to move in the direction of her or his origin that is the cosmic power or being.

In another context, matter has been supposed to be a base or a substratum on which all the rest can be reduced or on which all can be shown to depend. Mind or consciousness is supposed to be an emergent product and not as the original or basic stuff. Spiritualism or rather religious concern has been supposed to divert one's attention from the proper understanding of one's existence and the society in which one lives. Such a concern is supposed to lull the consciousness and make people passive and derive solace from fate when they are afflicted with the suffering. The class which is privileged one and has control over the means of production keeps the suffering class of have-nots in their fatal stupor of religion. It is in this sense that religion is called opium of the masses. Notwithstanding the theoretical conundrums, the idea of the disparity between the classes and the resulting idea of the inevitable clash between the two has changed the face of a large part of the world.

It should be noted that we are operating with a concept of matter which is now no more valid from the point of view of scientific understanding. So far as the common, day to day perception is concerned, most of us still use the term matter in the same old way. Thus what obstructs, what is inert, what is shapeless and solid or opaque – we call matter. It is now common knowledge that matter is supposed to be potentially a source of energy. Einstein has packed the idea in his well known formula $E=Mc2$. Thus mass and energy are convertible terms. On the other hand the life processes are ultimately traced to some chemicals and their interplay. The relation with life and food (a form of chemicals) had been recognized even in the ancient time. In *Taittirya Upanisad*, the rsi said *'annatapurusa'*, meaning 'made of food'. The individual is born out of *anna* - cereals. Similar ideas can be found in the *Chhandogya Upanisad* also. It is common knowledge that a person emaciated by hunger cannot perceive or think clearly. While some exceptions to such a relationship are also found, yet by and large it is true that for a healthy mind one needs a healthy body.

Though it has often been said, that all that human beings do, is determined by the thinking in mind, yet it is body which has to bear most of the burden of whatever bad, wrong, or evil human beings do. Senses are associated with body. Eyes, ears, nose, and skin are there to be noticed in the body. Feeling of satisfaction, satiety, and pleasure are connected with body. It is the body which feels cold or hot. Such feelings drive and move men. They repeatedly perform activities which bring them such feelings of pleasure. As has so often been noted, the agent, who has mainly her or his satisfaction in one's mind, is often oblivious of the inconvenience, pain or discomfort of the other. Thus human beings are driven to do even undesirable acts in order to have pleasure. Spiritualistic abhorrence or rejection of body (remember, some thinkers have gone on to say that body is the tomb of soul), because of the feelings of pleasure and enjoyment and consequent indifference and cruelty to body, ignores the crucial significance and meaning of body in the human existence.

Suppose there were no body and consequently no desire, then life and the world would have been impossible. Let us for a while try to see what possible significance can be attributed to body. Any one of us when thinks of oneself is thinking of one's embodied existence. Not merely a child but a grown up would think of his embodied existence when addressed by others. When I say there are things, there are other persons, then, it is because of my existence, that I can make such a distinction. I am thinking of myself as having a position somewhere and can regard things and persons as close or nearby or away or distant from me. When I have to pick up something or fetch it from some distance, it is because of the fact that the body is placed in a certain position, at a certain distance and it is because of the fact that the members of the body can move in a certain way. Nearness, distance, yesterdays, todays, tomorrows are all relative to my bodily existence. When it is said that, I grow or am growing, or I have a certain complexion, or height, young or old, or I am healthy or sick, then these are all bodily features that are being described. I am identified by some bodily feature, when it comes to legal identification. In fact, my legal person, which can be identified, held or released, punished or rewarded (think of the award stand on which the winners are placed), depend on my body. As someone said, one can imprison my body not my soul.

Without there being a concept of body, it is unthinkable of birth, growth, marriage, family, different people, their fighting or cooperating, acting or not acting, walking, sitting, sleeping, and innumerable such activities. It is because of desires, activities, and sufferings and pains that body is distinguished from spirit, soul, or mind, as if mind, soul or spirit had no role in sensations, perception, sufferings, and pleasures. On the contrary, without the mind or consciousness it would be impossible to have any feeling, desire, thinking of projects, and of course, of reflecting on the experience. Both body and mind have their roles in experience and action. Not realizing this composite contribution, and holding body alone as responsible for the ills of life, the main solution to all ills of life has been conceived in terms of realizing the separation of the spirit or atma from body. With the wash, baby is also thrown away.

It is not realized that doing good, which implies doing something for the other in material terms – caring in sickness, relieving the other of poverty, making shelters for the needy, not hurting someone, not giving pain or causing discomfort to someone, not killing; would be unimaginable if the others are not regarded as embodied beings. Thus if life and the world have to be accepted, and accept you must, the centrality of body will have to be granted. Let us come back to mind. As we noted that things first begin in mind. Let us also realize that while talking of mind we are not talking of something mysterious or of such a nature which is beyond language, and meaning. Notice, that we would often move our hand towards our forehead when we wish to point to our mind, or think of mind, or think of something which may be in our mind. That shows that unconsciously or without knowing we have accepted that our mind is placed somewhere in our head. In other words that it is a part of our body.

Thus to be conscious of some thought, feeling, or want is to find our brain and nervous system properly working. Someone is likely to raise a serious objection to what has been said here about the body. If body were really so important and so crucial to human existence and experience, then what happens when a person is dead. The body continues to be there, but it is found that the main functions which indicate life have come to an end. The body no more responds to any external stimulus. It stops seeing, hearing and so on. If it were by itself capable it could have continued to react or respond as before. That shows that there was something else which enabled the person to respond and act. This something else is also considered responsible for the life force. It was soul spirit or atma which has now left the body. It was because of the soul, spirit or atma that there was prana or life in the body. Once the atma left the body, the body became completely inert and inactive. In fact very soon it starts getting putrefied and it becomes necessary to dispose it off as early as possible.

It is now generally accepted that death is declared when brain has stopped working. Brain stops working in the absence of supply of oxygen. The heart also stops beating and the blood circulation ceases to function. In most cases no succour is either available or reaches the person and the person dies. Because of the advance of the science of medicine, it is now possible to remedy the defects afflicting the heart, and thereby maintain the supply of oxygen to brain. As is general knowledge, even heart transplants have become possible. In fact, various other vital organs, such as kidneys, liver, and even lungs are getting transplanted. It is generally found that after such medical interventions people who would have died are saved and are found to survive for quite some time. The search for genes responsible for decay and old age is on. The remarkable properties of stem cells which can supply the tissues otherwise decayed or dead have generated hopes for the cure of diseases like Parkinson and Alzheimer.

What can be said as a consequence of such medical interventions? Can death be pushed away, and indefinitely? Even if that is the case, does it in anyway affect the idea that it is because the *atma* or spirit has left the body that a man dies or has no more life. Is it not like correcting the function of a machine? Even, in the context of the machine there are limits to the procedure of correction. It cannot be kept working indefinitely with continuous corrections.

Given the fact, that medical intervention can correct the bodily mechanism to a very great extent and thereby push the death further and further, what implication such an intervention has for the concept of *atma* or spirit? In the absence of such intervention, *atma* would have left the body, does that mean that *atma* accepts and approves of such intervention? But could it not be the case that intervention is really an interference with the plans of *atma?* There are still more puzzling questions which have remained unattended so far. As we know *atma* has been defined as pure consciousness and if we go by the theory of Advait Vedanta, *atma* neither has desires nor does it act. It is a state being utterly distinct and different from anything that can be exemplified from the phenomenal realm. In such a case, the first question arises is how is it that *atma* allows itself to be trapped in the body which is at the most a polluting component? If it chooses to be there, why does it decide that on some particular moment it would leave this prison? If it has so decided, then nothing what to say of medical intervention, should be able to disrupt its plan.

If we move to a different usage of the term of atma or soul, where it is said to suffer, or enjoy, perhaps endowed with memory even then, may be, we are closer to the term jiva that obviously is closer to body, then is the transcendental entity called *atma* or soul. Life, consciousness, experience seem to make sense in the context of such a being which may be regulating or directing all our thoughts and activities. Since at times we act wrongly even commit sins, then could it be the same *jiva* or *atma* which regulates all our thoughts and actions? Greeks talked of an evil spirit which would lead the being in a wrong direction. In fact, a belief is prevalent in which every human being is supposed to be guided by two diametrically different forces – evil and the good. It is not clear if such a belief is compatible with human freedom. For if the guiding spirits are powerful and they alone influence our thinking and activities, then in that case we are no more than the play things of either of these spirits or forces.

These metaphysical or non-phenomenal aspects do not seem to be compatible with the actual life that people live on the earth. For the social structure, legal requirements, and political rights all presuppose beings with free will. They can be held responsible for what they do and not do. The argument, that I could not but commit sin, because I was under the sway of some evil spirit, would not hold water, in a court of law. These beliefs relating to separable *atma* or spirit are the legacy of ancient thinking and seem to be deeply engrained in human mind. Their epistemological and ontological validity is beyond rational grounds. They seem to be significant from the point of view of keeping human beings on the path of good conduct. For they point to a direction other than the phenomenal. Such a direction is prized because the phenomenal offers a mix treat, for a larger segment of humanity phenomenal offers mostly misery, suffering, and deprivation. Thus the transcendental orientation helps turning the gaze away from the phenomenal and thereby helps to bear the suffering.

As recognized and pointed out by social thinkers, such an orientation also turns away the gaze from the real source of human misery which is a consequence of certain kind of social structure, and largely man-made. Marxist or socialist thinking has been significant for it had insisted that it is because of a certain class in the society that the other class suffers. That is why Marx suggested philosophers to postpone understanding the world and try to change it. If the structural factors are largely consequences of human doings, their change or modification must also be within human volition. Unfortunately the actual moves in this direction have involved human suffering in a different way and form. Attempts at elimination of political rivals, forced concentration camps, wide distrust of citizens and making inroads into their privacy, continuous fear and insecurity have marked the transformational processes. Besides, the opportunists succeeded to make hay while it shone even in spite of the changing process.

This, however, brings us back to some inherent weaknesses with which most human beings suffer. We are back to desire, greed, possessiveness, indifference to the concern for the other, exploiting the other for one's own narrow ends and so on. Thus the crucial struggle has to be fought within one's own self. This should be true of each self. But the question as to the nature of this self again pops up. If the above discussion carries any weight, it seems to be clear that the self has to be understood in the context of this world. It has to be seen more as a person than some invisible, intangible, non-phenomenal and transcendental being away from the day to day concerns of human life.

Although the mind terminology would continue to be in usage, whatever progress is made in the brain research, it can also be shown that such a terminology actually functions within a larger vocabulary – a vocabulary which also includes terms applying to bodily features. Reflect on sentences such as these, 'this mango tastes good', 'the air is quite cold, please close the window', 'what a nice experience it was when we had that party yesterday', 'can you imagine how big a whale is', 'his words hurt me to the core', the law of identity can be illustrated by saying that A is A. 'since it is because of self, mind or consciousness that we are able to see, hear or taste, self, mind or consciousness cannot itself be seen, heard or tasted.' In the absence of either the mental vocabulary or the bodily vocabulary none of these sentences would make sense. Does it not indicate that life as lived or experienced cannot dispense with either the feeling aspect or the felt aspect? In other words both mental and physical go to make the human world. One might say, who denies this? The question really is that though both mental and physical is involved in life and experience how can we explain that they function in relation to each other.

But does such a problem arise if no separable, intangible and transcendental entity is postulated? Mental vocabulary indicates certain functions which may ultimately come to be related with brain physiology. It is also a fact that none of the terms used in the mental vocabulary be shown to have a correlative referent there. The search for a mind apart from a brain in the human body would be a vain search. The same could be said about consciousness or spirit or atma. If the words do not indicate any existing, identifiable part or whole within the body, then how do they come to have a meaning? This is true, that the words like feeling, thinking willing, imagining, remembering enable us to describe our experience, enable us to express ourselves. Anyone who hears them understands what is being said and what sense to make of it. One can even try to explain any of these terms to a being who does not understand our language at all, by doing something or moving in a certain way. Suppose I want to convey, look I am feeling pain here on my arm, then I may take over the hand of my interlocutor and press it uncomfortably on his arm and tell him, well, that is what I mean. Thus there remains nothing mysterious about these terms. If someone asks who feels, I may move my finger towards myself pointing to my whole person and that does the trick. So it is I, the person who feels. There ends the business.

Both the terms – mind and matter are used in several contexts and their meaning remains to be perfectly intelligible without causing any puzzlement. 'Mind your business', 'Let me give him a bit of my mind', 'Would you mind if I sit here', 'Please don't mind, he is just a child', 'She has propounded a wonderful theory, a great mind indeed', 'Well, what is the matter', 'It does not matter, don't bother about it much', 'We had to discuss a very important matter', 'Never mind for it does not matter', are some of the examples of the sentences in which both the terms mind and matter are used in various interesting ways. These usages do not suggest any metaphysical problem. But they do show that mind and matter after all are not disparate as a tradition has made them out to be.

It would be interesting and instructive to reflect on the phenomenon of yoga. A distinctively Indian contribution, yoga is based on the insight that the bodily functions can be brought under voluntary control. In yoga we are told about the close relationship between a certain bodily posture and a corresponding mental state. We should rather say that being in a certain bodily posture is also to be in a certain sort of feeling state. This shows that matter and mind or body and spirit are two sides of the same coin. It might be argued that yoga is not merely a matter of posture. This is true. But yoga involves the practice of concentration or *dhyana* and *dhyana* requires the aspirant to be in a certain bodily posture. In 'Sadhanpada' of Patanjali *Yoga Sutra*, eight steps are recommended – *yama, niyama, aasana, pranayama, pratyahara, dharana, dhyana* and *Samadhi*. We need not go into their detail but we should notice that besides mental effort they also require bodily controls. Such controls are supposed to help in attaining a certain sort of state of mind. Thus the whole procedure of yoga depends on the intimate relationship between mind and body.

In the brief account above, we have noticed that the terms mind, consciousness, *atma*, spirit, *jiva*, body and matter have subtle distinctions in their usage and they are not carefully distinguished from each other in the common parlance. We have also noticed that the water tight compartment between mind and body is based on not realizing the role of both in the human experience adequately. Besides, the controversy relating to the relation between mind and brain is alive and remains so far unsettled. Though, the indications seem to point to more and more revelations regarding the functions of brain and the notion of mind receding into background.

Individual and Society

"The main uniform effect of calamities upon political and social structure of society is an expansion of governmental regulation, regimentation and control of social relationships and a decrease in regulation and management of social relationships by individuals and private groups." Pitrim Alexandrovich Sorokin.

One can point to someone and say 'here is a person' or 'here is the individual about whom I have been talking to you'. But one cannot point to something and then say 'this is the society to which I belong'. Individuals can be located in a spatio-temporal frame. They can be photographed. One can touch them and hold them. One can speak to them and can also listen to them. But these things cannot be done so far as 'society' is concerned. It is however, possible to talk about some specific society in a spatio- temporal frame. For example, one can talk about the Indian society in the twentieth century. Obviously, the Indian society will have to be located on the Indian sub-continent. There are Indians living elsewhere in countries other than India. They are referred to as 'Diaspora' as a whole.

The term 'society' is used as a collective noun. But it does not refer to some specific group of people in a fixed and determined spatio-temporal frame only. The term as a noun refers to a group of people whose membership remains in a fluid state. Moreover a society is not a statuary body which is constituted by the consent of some specific individuals entering into a club with some rules and regulations at some point of time. It comes to be formed in an automatic and natural way. We often talk about a society, as if it were a statuary body and had rules and regulations. Not only this, the term inhabits in our consciousness in such a way as if it refers to some super entity which is capable of overseeing what we do and think, and also what we ought to be doing and not doing, something like a super-ego. In fact, we are told that super-ego in the psychic structure represents the voice of society, while id represents the un-organized instinctual store house.

It might be said that Indian society comprises of various communities determined as caste groups. Each community can be seen as having all the features which could be generally associated with a society itself. Over a period a community comes to develop some rules and regulations spelling out the norms of behaviour of its members. Some communities may also have these rules and regulations in written form. When we think of Hindu community we also think of the various texts known as 'Dharma Sastras' which contain such rules, regulations and norms. As things are, not all members of the community are aware or acquainted with these texts, though they may have heard about them. It also follows that not all members of the community follow the rules prescribed in these texts in a conscious way. Most people go by conventions as they are passed on from generation to generation to be followed in their families by their elders.

It should be noted that it is not possible to follow such rules just as they are found in the written form for two reasons, first, because the rules were framed in certain conditions and in some cases were specific to the circumstances in which they were visualized; secondly, there being more than one text and these texts having scribed by different writers, they obviously contain commands which may be disparate with each other. Anyone who would follow a text in order to regulate one's behaviour will have to make a choice, which would be her or his choice. Such a thing happens in rare cases. Generally, as we have noted, people go by conventions of their families.

The reality of the idea of society or community or as we call it *samaj,* can be understood in terms of its impact or effect on our consciousness when we think or act. When I seem to choose something and at the same time I also have an apprehension in my mind as to how the community would look at it or assess my action, the notion of community acquires a reality as a force which I have to reckon with. I may not care about the community, I may defy it, I may resist or rebel against it, or I may just go by what I take to be the recommendations of the community, in all these cases, the idea of community or *samaj* occurs to be active in my awareness and that indicates its reality. Thus while the idea of a community or *samaj* may not have referent like the term 'individual', yet it cannot be said to be imaginary or a fiction for that reason.

In a sense the reality of the community or samaj is much more ominous and obsequious as compared to the individual. Individuals come and go, community remains. In the form of a regulative force it can be seen as the career of culture and tradition which determine its profile. It is from such a background that an individual, consciously or unconsciously, derives her or his ideals and projects. As a result an individual looks to the members of the community for appreciation of what s/he does or achieves. The consequent emotional impact either boosts the confidence of the individual or dampens her or his enthusiasm depending on success or failure. Even the modes of resistance, opposition or combat are formed by the background beliefs which have their origin in the community itself.

Thus, it may be the idea of the community, the ways of thinking and acting of the seniors or elders in the community and the available codes of rules and regulations which have their impact on the individual in one way or the other, consciously or unconsciously. Whether it is ideas relating to the division of society into the four varnas, or the unity of all beings, or the belief that it is not the membership of a varna that gives identity to an individual but his actions and deportment, that one should fight for justice and oppose injustice, or the kind of proper objectives worth following, the evil tendencies which have to be avoided or overcome and similar guiding principles can be traced to one text or the other in the vast literature that is there so far as the Indian society is concerned. Similar statements would hold for any other community or society with necessary modifications.

It should be noted that the impact of the community differs from one type of habitat to the other. Major distinction can be noted between rural and urban, tribal or mainstream. Social distances are more rigid in rural communities, but then it also depends how a village is connected with a township. Tele-gadgets being available in a village or the village being close in the vicinity of a township, the physical distances are gradually neutralized. Yet, in a major way, the cohesiveness in spite of the fact of the social distance is greater in a village as compared to an urban habitat. Thus the ways of living in a village are more conservative and coercive as compared to those of a city. While the pockets of power in the village structure have their own impact on the style of life and mutual relationships, in city their function though present but is diffused. The consciousness of an ordinary individual in a village is more intensely aware of the force of community then that of an ordinary individual in a city. A tribal community, perhaps, is not characterized by the social distances in the same way as is a village community.

Because the gradually increasing mobility between various kinds of habitats, increasingly gradual introduction of electronic gadgets in rural areas, spread of non-governmental organizations and their work in the rural areas and arrival of media to a certain extent are introducing changes of all sort in the village life. Thus the awareness of an individual in a village is undergoing a change though it is slow and not radical. There is no doubt that the community largely determines the ways of thinking and actions of individuals, individuals in their turn affect the profile of the community. It is to be noted that without individuals there can be no community or society. While without the idea of a community there can be no order or structure in a group of individuals.

The conservative ways of a society often generate tensions and conflicts when new situations and new demands lead the individuals in different directions. We have already noticed that owing to occupational mobility, difficulties encountered in housing in case of large families in the old houses, and differences of dispositions in the members of the same family have led to smaller families and a spread out of the members of family in distant locations. Differences in occupations, in fortunes, in success and achievements have also divided the members of family. Impersonalism and indifference to the concerns of others have grown in such a way that people have become distant to each other even if they live together. Individuals are growing more self-centred and confined to their own interests and projects coupled with an indifference to the interests or needs of the other.

Individuals may have genuine grievances against the community when conservatism and rigidity of traditions in a community fail to help the individuals in meeting new demands and necessities. Choice of career, choice of profession, choice of a spouse, choice of living in a certain way, often come in conflict with the established traditional modes of a community. Individuals come into conflict with each other because there are individuals who claim to voice the tradition and community and there are individuals who have to find new and different solutions to their problem.

The funny thing is that the elders or seniors who now claim to be the authority and harbingers of the tradition had in their own youth undergone a similar conflict with their elders and seniors. Once they attain the status of the seniors they become oblivious of their own youth and youthful ways and consequently fail to appreciate the aspiration of the new generation. In this scenario, the notions of order, justice, values, and worthy life become fluid and debatable.

This conflict infects the whole society. Debates and controversies become the order of the day. Unfortunately the matters do not remain confined around the table only. Controversies and conflicts relating to order, justice and values can be seen as originating from different sources. We have already noted the generation gap. If we go deeper in the issue of generation gap we may be able to identify the other and perhaps the real origin of such conflicts. Let us, therefore, try to probe the matter of generation gap a little further. Let us ask the question whether the perception of values as related to elders and as related to the younger generation really varies.

Let's take for example the incidents of honour killings in certain states of our country. Generally what happens is that the members of one family do not favour the proposed wedding of their offspring with the offspring of the other family. The members of the other family also think the same way. It is possible that in some cases family of the one side may be inclined to favour the leaning of their son or daughter. The reasons generally adduced for the rejection of relationship have either to do with the same gotra (the clan identity), or differences in the castes – which may be of the same status or may not be of the same status. Besides, there may be some vested interest involved such as relating to property or money or status, or some hostility existing between the two families.

The reasons we have noticed are not all of the same kind. Some have to do with the understanding of genetics, caste structure, and status, while the other has to do with personal interests or feelings. When no specific controversy or conflict is involved, we find everybody talking about the brotherhood and equality of all beings. It is obvious that there are contradictions involved in the different kind of considerations and the general beliefs as held in the community. Now let us have a look on the feelings and the consideration of the young people who want to live together. Often it is a matter of physical infatuation for each other, without any regard to the mutual compatibility in respect of temperaments, abilities, and future projects. But this may not be the case. The couple may have mutual acquaintance for long and may be convinced of the mutual compatibility which would enable them to live a long a happy life together. They may of course, fall back on the general principle of the equality of all people and thus may disregard the caste and status distinctions. These later considerations may lead them to think of the unfairness or injustice of the opinion and commands of their elders.

Now, so far as the general principle of equality and brotherhood is concerned, we find everybody believes it, at least, theoretically. But as we notice the considerations of caste and status intervene and the general principle is thrown to winds. So far as the matter of genetics is concerned that becomes a controversial issue which is better taken to the arena of experts. It is obvious that elders turn the issue as damaging their prestige or because of the hostility which exists between the families the issue is taken be a matter of honour and valour. These considerations, obviously are not based on moral principles, but on the unpleasant background and die-hard attitudes. If the elders ignore the earlier unpleasant background, and do not make the extraneous considerations into a moral issue and bring open and broader attitude to have its play, and if the younger people are not merely under the magic charm of physical infatuation, and have really assessed the issue with the considerations necessary for a long and happy companionship, then there is a likelihood of there being a different picture emerging. Things would not result into violent incidents.

Thus it appears, that the origin of the conflict lies in the deviation from or the diffusion of the age old principle of brotherhood and equality of mankind on the one hand and the confusion and blurring of the vision by the false values of money and status which also underlie the caste divisions.

There is another serious situation which can be seen as generating the grounds of conflict. An individual is a member of a family. But she is also a member of institutions other than family. These institutions are of different types according to their goals and functions. Some provide support to the traditions and structure of the society. They differ from community to community. Some provide a grid for the political fabric of the society, for example, a democratic set up. Some provide occupations and employment to the population. There are others which provide skills, information and knowledge to the growing members of the society. An individual as a member of each of these institutions has duties and rights towards each of them.

Loyalties to these different institutions on the one hand and loyalty to any one of them and one's own freedom of thought on the other do sometime present difficult situations within which it becomes difficult for the individual to decide as to what course of action should one follow. Whether it is cultural institution, occupational institution or political institution conflicting situations arise.

We have already noted an example from the cultural institution in terms of honour killings. We have also noticed that because of occupational exigencies, size of the family, changes have modified the structures, and inter-relationships within the family. These changes introduce differences in opinion and ways of thinking and consequently generate tensions and conflicts. Changes can also be noticed in religious rituals, in the manner of observance of festivals, and also in the wedding ceremonies. These changes are more pronounced in urban life, rather than in the rural life. Marriage ceremonies used to be spread on several days some decades back, but now they are all completed in a day or so. Funeral ceremonies were also performed spreading till thirteen days. Now the period has come to be shortened to three days. Visits to temples, or sacred places have come to be radically dropped. The manner in which festivals were observed is undergoing gradual changes in many respects. For example the accidents occurring while children fly kites, or when the fire crackers are exploded, have necessitated greater care in kite flying, and exploding the fire crackers.

It is very likely that the changing demands are disregarded by some individuals while there may be insistence to take them into consideration by others. These conflicting attitudes may introduce tension and conflicts in inter-personal relationships. That may also happen between those who live in neighborhood. In occupational institutions individuals generally follow the ways of their occupation as dictated by the employers. But there may be individuals who may find it difficult to go strictly by all those rules and regulations which are imposed on them by the system. This factor is taken into account in the managerial strategies and subordinates are being treated with some dignity and their views and ideas are often invited to be considered so that better involvement could be induced. However, in smaller units and in vast areas the subordinates have to work like cogs in the machine.

Such conditions are bound to create tensions and conflicts among the workers. One need not talk about the approach of the employer or the capitalist whose interest is confined to the maximization of profit and an indifference to the needs and concerns of the workers employed by him. There are of course, individual circumstances in which things may differ from case to case. But in general the relation between the employer and the employee is well known and its state is far from what it ought to be.

In the political institutions, the main source of conflict may be found in the party organization and the individual as a member of the party. It is very often the case that the individual members hold different opinions in opposition to the general policy of the party. In some cases the party discipline does not permit any deviation from what the high command thinks or decides. As is well known, the left parties and some right parties have had stricter discipline in this respect than some other parties. However, consider any party, individuals would be found who do not see eye to eye with the authority in the party. The reasons for differences may be genuine and rational though they some time are dictated by personal interest. Whatever may be the case, an individual may find oneself in a situation in which either one defies the party whip and walks out or goes by whatever s/he is told to accept.

In general, the problem arises when an individual is conscious of being a member of an institution and therefore being loyal to its objectives, projects, policy and the rules of discipline on the one hand, and is also conscious of the ideas which apparently seem to be in conflict with the explicit and declared aims and policy of the institution but appear to the individual to be in the interest of the institution in the longer run. Such a conflict may assume a serious dimension if the conflicting ideas are backed by good reasons and are completely independent of any narrow interest of the individual herself or himself. Such a thing may happen, when new or unexpected demands arise and the leaders refuse to recognize their significance for the institution and some other members begin to realize that a different approach or strategy needs to be adopted to meet the different and new situation.

One of the things that seem to impress on the mind of people is that once you have adopted certain objectives, and also have decided how to attain them, then there should be no deviation from the decisions taken and everybody should stick to whatever has been decided. While such an approach seems to be reasonable and necessary for the fulfillment of any objective, yet it may so happen, that some significant consideration has escaped notice, and its neglect at some point of time may become a hurdle in the fulfillment of the objective, hence it becomes necessary for someone to bring that point to the notice of all concerned. Unfortunately, the feeling of ego enters into the situation and members fail to see the reason just because each one is swayed or persuaded by the rightness of her or his point of view. History reveals that the consequences of such conflict result into a schism and a new party or institution comes to be formed. This has happened in all kinds of institutions.

There is another side of such conflicting situations. Institutions are careers and protectors of certain norms and standards which are supposed to guide the actions and behaviour of the members. These norms and standards can also be seen as describing positive ethics or morality. This is specifically true of cultural institutions. Before moving further let us notice a distinction between two kinds of norms. There are norms which are universal in their generality. Doing good, speaking truth, not stealing or killing, keeping promises, are some such norms. They are recommended in all societies and in all times. On the other hand there are more specific guide lines relating to type of clothes to be worn, type of food to be consumed, type of general behaviour towards others, types of rituals to be performed on certain occasions and so on. These later differ from people to people. A close investigation of such rules would reveal that most of them came into existence because of local needs determined by the local conditions. Somehow, people continue to stick to them even when the local conditions have undergone changes, or the locale has itself changed.

The new conditions require different kind of guiding rules, which when introduced create conflict with the already accepted ones. Traditions are a great help in guiding largely the behaviour and ways of living of a people. But it is also necessary that from time to time wise people reflect on the traditions and modify them according to the new requirements. Such an attitude would require a critical scrutiny of the prevailing positive morality. People debate the basis on which critical scrutiny could be carried through. Often these debates generate tensions between individuals and the institutions to which they belong.

It may be debated whether the so-called new demands are genuine and whether the new thinking is not a way to support individual deviations which hide momentary attachments of the individuals. Individuals or the members belonging to new generation might think of the older generation as having a rigid and dogmatic attitude or being authoritative and egoistic and blind to the genuine needs of the new generation. Thus the question arises, how such a disparity of opinions can be resolved. As already noted such a conflict is not a new phenomenon but can be seen as the characteristic of any two generations in any period.

If a proper dialogue is to be instituted between the generations, several conditions need be fulfilled. The involved members will have to take care that they are free from the pressure of 'I' on the one hand and have a genuine eye, and an open mind in respect of the issue in question. They have to be inspired by a sincere and intense wish to come to a resolution. They have to treat each other with due dignity and have to entertain the opposed view with objectivity and dispassionately.

An individual need to be aware of the fact, that her or his identity cannot be located out of the network within which s/he exists and has to live through. Each of us has to exist or live through with or amongst others. It is true in our feelings, thinking and in our decision each of us is alone. But each of us owes a major segment of one's thoughts, one's language, one's aspirations and projects, even the ways of resistance and dissent to the society, tradition, and culture to which one belongs. Even our freedom has a meaning within the co-existence defined by the people with whom we live. It is responsibility, the other side of the coin, which links our freedom with the freedom of others. Thus individuality as totally disconnected with other beings is drained off all its content.

I and the Other

"My relationship with the Other as neighbor gives meaning to my relations with all the others."
Emmanuel Levinas

Well, what could be more obvious, clear and certain than 'I'?

What could be closer to me than 'I'? And yet 'I' poses numerous problems some of which seem to be so riddled that no clear understanding seems to be in sight. When I think of myself, what do I find? I may look towards myself, that is, I may stoop a little and try to look at myself. I may find myself as getting fatty, or needing better wears. If I close my eyes and I try to look inward as they say, I may find myself entertaining some thoughts of visiting a place or a person or reading a book or perhaps some other such errand. Or I may be recalling some experience I had in past which has left either a bad taste or perhaps some pleasant memory which I can enjoy at the moment. Or maybe I am not feeling very comfortable, perhaps it is too cold or perhaps it is too hot and so on. Or maybe I am not happy with myself for I did something which now I find was either foolish, or undesirable, or sinful. I may be asking myself how could it be that I did what I did. I may be looking for some excuse which would lessen the burden of my guilt. There are thousand and one things that I could be feeling, thinking or doing(for example, trying to recall or trying to solve some problem and so on) when I peep into myself.

It is clear that I can think about myself, I can look towards myself; I can be even angry or be pleased with myself. Does that mean that there exists another 'I', which I confront? There is, of course, the I which I had been, there is the I which I am and there is going to be the I which I will become. Sometime I let myself go and the 'I' emerges naturally. Sometime, I wish to be something. I want to become something or somebody. I wish to conform to some ideal image – an image of a wealthy or powerful or famous someone or perhaps some mendicant. It is clear then that what I want to be, I am not. Someone might suggest that I could be only what I am. How could it be that 'I am' and also that 'I am not'? But what would it mean to say that I become what I really am? I am often told by wise men that I have really forgotten my real being and should try to find out my real self. I am also told that I have lot of potentialities and I should actualize them. The potentiality to which wise men point out may not be what normally we understand by potentialities – say becoming a painter, or a musician, or a leader, or some such thing which I am not at the moment. Now this seems to be clear that 'I' or for that matter its content is not a simple affair to decipher or describe.

There is another interesting complexity in trying to understand what 'I' am. Often I am in two minds when confronted with a choice. Some time I have a conflict in my mind amongst different ideas relating to some decision. Such situations imply that behind the supposed 'I' there are more 'I's'. This sounds funny and non-sense. But we hear of abnormalities such as 'split personality'. When one suffers with an affliction of this kind one behaves in opposite ways without having the awareness that one is so behaving. That shows that in such cases two persons inhabit the same body. Could it be the case that there is some kind of integrating function which helps in resolving the conflicts or tensions that one suffers from? This suggests that though we have experiences normal or abnormal when we find ourselves in uncertain dilemmas which seem to indicate more than one beings in our one body but there is also an 'I' which enables us to get over such conflicts and showing that in fact there is only one 'I' and not more than one.

According to the Vedant tradition/s there is something basically wrong with most of us. We have forgotten our real selves. We do not actually know who we are. In the absence of right understanding of ourselves, we confuse ourselves with our bodies. This is supposed to be fundamental ignorance of which I am a victim. Till I get rid of this ignorance and false understanding, I am not going to be what I really am. This is not an easy thing to understand. One has to undergo an extensive training which allows one to see what is what. It is then that it gradually dawns on me that I am not my body. I have it but I am not it. I am distinct from it. It is body that suffers pain and pleasure. It is bodily existence which has to do things and face the struggle of life and so on. As atman I have nothing to do with any of these things. I am pure consciousness and pure bliss. It is body that comes into existence and one day it becomes lifeless and useless. I am neither born nor shall 'I' die. Some contest this view but by and large many *sanatanies* (those who are traditionalists, but what really is the tradition?) tend to accept it.

However, though most people accept it, yet few seem go by it. This understanding does not seem to affect their thinking, acts and projects at all. This discrepancy marks our life in general and we are not bothered about it. Right now, I am not concerned with the ramifications and consequences of such a discrepant living. I am trying to think about 'I'. There is such a view that 'I' is radically different from what is generally understood by it. We have such a thing as census. Everyone would be approached by some government official to record everything about oneself. But the census form does not contain any column in which the individual be asked about his real self – or the self which is not a body. In practice there is no need to think of a real 'I' or self as apart from the individual person counted by the census men.

Confining this discussion for the time being to the 'I' which is going to be counted and whose details would be recorded by the census person, it would be noticed that this 'I' is identifiable in the legal sense and in the context of day to day living, can be located at some time or place, can be met and talked to, can be asked to do something or help or cooperate in some venture, has ideas, expectations, memories, feelings, projects, and besides has relationship with many other similar beings. Such an 'I' may be a female, child, teen or an old person. It is clear, that the way such a person would regard oneself, and the way others would regard this person, would spell out the profile of such a person.

It is in this context, that each person is distinguished from every other one. It is the embodiment that marks out one person from the other. It is also because of being embodied that one can be located somewhere at some time. Each person has to have one's identity and for this purpose identity documents have acquired importance. Identity is seen in more than one context. There is the identity from the legal point of view, so that person can be recognized. Identity may also indicate the social position of an individual. There is the identity that the individual feels as being different from any other individual. Identity is also related to an achievement or a series of achievements that distinguish a person from a mass of other people.

Looked at from the subjective point of view identity has posed a problem for the philosophers. Every time an individual thinks or utters 'I', it is supposed that the various instances of 'I'; refer to the same 'I'. The question that philosophers have been trying to solve has been how can it be ascertained that the various occurrences of 'I' refer to the same 'I'. The question becomes more significant when it is realized that the person who utters 'I' is a changing entity in respect of thoughts, feelings, actions and even in the context of body. The cells that constitute our bodies are undergoing constant change. Moreover, in certain abnormal states the individuals may suffer from a split personality, as the famous story of Jekyll and Hyde illustrates. It is also a fact that each individual is constantly in the process of growth and later in the process of decay. Sometime a person herself or himself may wonder whether she or he is the same person that she or he had been, particularly when the person had performed some extraordinary act –good or bad.

Our discussion thus far seems to suggest the existence of a person within a person, an 'I' within an 'I'. Kant, a great German thinker, believed that the 'I' which an individual pronounces in successive sentences that one utters, is an analytical 'I'.(If 'x is y' is an analytical statement, then y says nothing about x. The statement amounts to saying that 's is s'). But repeated occurrences of x as 'I' need to be related with each other and thus being analytical, different occurrences of 'I' require a synthetic principle and such a principle has been called by him as the 'transcendental unity of apperception' meaning roughly some transcendental self which can never appear as an object. In contrast to such a view there is a belief that to think that there is a stable self or an identical self, which is immune to any change, is to think of something as false. There is no self that is constant or stable. In fact, such a self does not exist. There is a continuity of mental events occurring one after the other, and this continuity is mistakenly understood as the constant self. As the reader would recollect such a concept was advanced by the Buddhists and was called *'anattavada'*.

Often the term ego is used for 'I'. This is a Greek word. The term ego has often been used in a pejorative way. It is not an appreciable quality in an individual to have an ego. The Sanskrit counterpart of ego is *'ahamkara'*. *Ahamkara* is supposed to be a consequence of false knowledge or ignorance and is supposed to distort the integration of personality. It is associated with undue pride, distinguishes a person from other individuals in an asymmetric and unnatural way. It is a heady concept and misleads the individual into a delusion of being superior to everyone else and hence in a position to rule over others. Ego also leads to stubbornness and makes the individual dogmatic. The line between ego and will is very thin. Not to have ego does not mean to be spineless and lack of confidence.

It is said that one must have confidence in one self in order to perform acts and duties successfully. But to have confidence and to be egoistic are two different kind of dispositions. While one is a necessary condition for performing a difficult deed, egoistic tendency may become a barrier in understanding the situation in a proper way. With a wrong perception one may succeed accidentally but normally the individual is likely to go in a wrong direction. Confidence requires a proper understanding of self and the task at hand.

As long as an individual remains concerned with her or his own projects and the projects do not involve any harm to the other or reaction or expectation from the other, no problem arises. But the individual often has expectations or apprehensions in respect of the other, and also imagines about the possible reactions – good or bad, of the other. Speculations about the other are influenced by the image that one has of the other and the way one thinks of the relationship with the other. In fact, most of one's life experiences are filled with the apprehensions of all kind which relate to the other. Philosophers have discussed about the relationship between 'I' and 'other', for such a relationship defines the human situation in a fundamental way.

Such a relationship comes to be determined by how I perceive myself as to what I am and what I take to be the other as to what s/he is. My image for myself seems to be definite and stable just as I regard the image of the other as definite and stable. But this seems to be deceptive. For though at a certain moment images appear to be stable yet a close observation would reveal that these images refer to beings that undergo constant change, which is often not perceptible. Few of us appear to be conscious of this fact of change which remains imperceptible. The other question is how the images come to be formed. When I think of myself I am often oblivious of that part which is contributed by what others think about me. Consciously or unconsciously my image of what I am is constituted by what others say about me. Though not everything that others think about myself, is accepted but much of it is. Others may think ill of me or may think well of me and it is not clear what part gets assimilated within the image I have of myself and how. This much is clear that part of 'I' is constituted by 'me' (or the image others have about me).

It should be noted that what others think about me is not always the same and may keep on changing depending on how they find me behaving with them or reacting to them and what they expect from me. Similarly my projects, objectives, and demands on the one hand and the degree of the confidence that I have in my capacity to carry through my goals determine my own image for myself. Since these projects do not remain the same always and since my capacity and ability to carry them through also does not remain stable, the image that I have of myself may not match with these and yet I may continue to think of myself in terms of a stable image.

My projects and my confidence may be so overwhelming that I may not suspect any weakness or drawback which might block or delay the fulfillment of these projects at a later date. I may not have assessed properly my capacities or abilities in respect of these projects. The consequence may be frustration and anger. It may either be directed towards my own self or I may find other people or circumstances interfering with my designs and efforts. The success story may, of course, move in a different direction.

Turning our discussion towards the second of the duo, that is, the 'other' the ramifications are no simpler.

In my dealings with the other, as is already pointed out, it depends how I think about the other, what image I have of the other. The images often serve as stereotypes and come to determine my reaction. The fact of the matter may be that the referent of these images may not remain the same over a period of time because of the changing circumstances. We normally do not expect any change in the other and think that we shall encounter exactly the same person when we encounter her or him next. Taking ourselves as stable and static entities we continue to interact with each other. Trust or distrust, belief or disbelief, like or dislike, faith or doubt, love or hate, may determine how we behave with each other. How we come to have trust or distrust, belief or disbelief, like or dislike, faith or doubt, love or hate in respect of the other person depends on what has happened earlier, what kind of experiences we have had already amongst ourselves.

It may be asked who do we refer to when we mention the word 'other'. Simple answer is one who is 'not I'. But simple answer does not help always. Clearly 'not I; is a class having infinite number of beings. They include family members, neighbours, friends, colleagues – senior or junior, and many others. What about animals or plants? Some time we have pets and we also grow plants. Do we have some kind of relation with them? Some people treat their pets just as their members and some have similar feelings for the plants that they grow. Besides, there are strangers, aliens and foreigners.

How do we relate ourselves to members of these different categories? We are scared or apprehensive or suspicious of those whom we do not know, that is, strangers. But such a reaction is not always inevitability. Much depends on our own personality make up, our experience with them and our information span. We may behave in a similar way with those whom we know and to whom we are close. I may suspect my wife, be apprehensive of my neighbor, or doubt the faithfulness of a friend. The narration of causes would be unmanageable and fortunately it is not necessary to go into it for most of us are aware of them. However, it would help to bring to mind of two points. First, relations based or caused by fear, apprehension, suspicion and undue expectations cannot be comfortable or happy. The second point is we suffer from fear, apprehension and suspicion because we do not think of the other as we think of ourselves.

One of the things which I am compelled to do is to accommodate the other within the space in which I myself am. So long as I am alone in my room I may move in any way I like, or do whatever I choose to do, though once again within the given constraints. For instance, I have to move within the four walls of my room, or I can do things only with the material that is available to me. Besides, I should be in the proper health and I should also be equipped with proper know how. I may consume what is available to me if I am hungry or thirsty or even otherwise. Now imagine someone enters my room. The situation does not remain the same. My freedom is now in some sense and to some extent comes to be curtailed. Much depends on who the person is. It also depends whether we two can stay on for a while in the room.

It is not merely a matter of sharing a space or time or some material, but also that of sharing thoughts, projects, jokes, or things of certain kind. The character of such sharing would depend on the prior acquaintance, on the extent of acquaintance, on the type of relationship which we have developed or going to develop. In fact, the presence of the other changes the whole world so far as I am concerned. But perhaps all this is merely an abstraction, or perhaps concerns a stage when it is possible for me to stay away from others in my lonely den having little to do with them. But it may not be possible for me to remain alone for a long time. The fact, on the contrary, is that the individual finds herself or himself with others right from the time one comes into the world. Existentialist philosophers have often drawn attention to being-in-the-world or being-with-others.

As life story of an individual unfolds it involves important characters other then the individual, if no one else, at least one's mother. One has to learn to be with the other, in fact, one learns right in the beginning how important and essential the other is for one's own existence. The idea of the other enters into one's awareness with the idea of one's own being as an individual. As I become aware of my 'I-ness' I also become aware of there being 'others'. The experiences in the beginning of the story usually involve the help and love one receives from others. Obviously this is a stage in which the individual as a child is not capable of doing anything for the other except the fact that its mere being or well being itself is considered to be one of the most precious happening. Who would remain unaffected when confronted with a child full of smile. It has often been valued as the most joyous of moments. The support or help a child receives in the early stages should be the source of the awareness of love and concern which make life worthwhile. The feeling of love and concern that the child has received hardly creates the feeling of otherness so far as the other individuals are concerned. The feeling of otherness related with the other individuals emerges and develops later when we come in contact with people who we are not acquainted with. Strangeness and otherness often go together. Often, the feeling of confronting stranger generates the feeling of insecurity, which may or may not decrease as we come to know the stranger better. In fact, mutual understanding, and mutual trust are likely to create a friendly relation which may last or may stay on for some time.

The desire of exclusive possession of the resources on the one hand and similarly the desire to be unique or being a hero often creates a wedge between the human relations. It is tragic that the kind of experiences which one had in one's childhood are more or less erased and one comes to be occupied more and more with suspicion, tension and hostility so far as the other is concerned. One gradually becomes more and more distrustful, scary, insecure and uneasy in the presence of the other.

If one goes by the advice as offered in one of the most significant upanisad – *Isa,* one may be able to get rid of such uncomfortable feelings and may be able to live in the world and with others relatively peacefully. In Isa, we are advised to treat the entire existence as pervaded by the presence of Isa – who governs the existence, and not to look at the possession of the other with greed, and thus enjoy the world for hundred years. Clearly, it is the idea of exclusive ownership which is at the root of fear, tension and insecurity. Rid of it, and enjoy and be happy.

Thus the relationship between the other and my self turns on the feeling of otherness as strangeness as well as on the feeling of possession and power. Getting rid of the feeling of otherness is not getting rid of the other. The other is as unique as I think I am. Leibnietz – a European thinker believed that if the two entities have the same attributes or properties they are not really two but one and propounded his theory of monads. He conceived each monad as different from the other. This view is compatible with the uniqueness of each individual. The life history of one individual differs from the life history of the other. Each individual has experiences which are in totality different from the experiences of the other individual. As human beings individuals may have similar potentialities. But different potentialities actualize in different individuals in different ways. Thus each individual is distinguished from the other in some important and distinctive feature. Each individual contributes to the richness of the whole in one's own distinctive way.

Most of us have a tendency to like or appreciate a person who conforms to our expected image of that person. The image of the other person in our mind is some time determined by the place that we think that person has in the social structure to which s/he belongs. It is also determined by the social distance that lies between us and the person concerned. Thus if a person is close to us we tend to like her or him if her or his ideas and practices are the ones with which we tend to agree. If the other occupies a position which is in some sense subordinate to us, we tend to think that her or his ideas cannot be mature or of a certain standard and naturally her or his practices would also be of an inferior order. The examples can be multiplied.

On the other hand, we are told that every individual should be treated as equal to the other. Most religions preach brotherhood amongst mankind. Unfortunately each religion seems to restrict this principle to its own adherents. The law in most civilized country is based on the equality of the citizens. Yet the labyrinthine procedures involved in the implementation of legal judgments often disregard this basic principle. If the judiciary is influenced by the political power or some other extraneous cause, then again this principle is disregarded. Even the socialist systems have not been able to go fully by the requirement of the principle of equality. Let us keep in mind that individuals cannot be equal in all respects. Thus what is demanded in terms of equality is equal distribution of opportunities, resources, and acceptance of the dignity of a person as a person. Acceptance of mutual regard of personhood amongst the individuals is one of the basic conditions of proper human relationship and communication. For example in the relationship of communication, listening is as much important as speaking. To listen is to regard the other with proper attitude and due respect. But the notion of equality and the necessity of recognizing the dignity of the person do not mean disregarding the uniqueness of the individual. Two individuals may be unique in several ways. They may think differently, they may act differently, they may have different goals and different projects and of course, they may have different capabilities and abilities. Yet they may respect each other as a person, they may enter into a dialogue with each other. It is not necessary that the dialogue may end in agreement. But this does not mean that they cannot sit around the same table and cannot share other experiences. Mutual disagreement does not exclude the possibility of some common ground.

To treat the individual as same as any other and to treat one as unique in some respect appear to be two opposed demands. But they are based on the notion of freedom. If my freedom is to be granted and respected, I should grant and respect the freedom of the other as well. But what does this mutual recognition of each other's freedom imply? If I consider the other person in some way as of a low order because s/he thinks in a way or has thoughts with which I do not agree, I am refusing to accept her or his freedom to think. If I think of the style of the living of the other person in derisive terms, I am not granting her or him the freedom to live in her or his own way. But does it mean that any silly, absurd or obscene idea should be accepted and people are permitted to have it? Does it mean that people are allowed to adopt malpractices and live in a way which is harmful for others and the society?

If the notion of equality and freedom lead to such absurd consequences, then either something is wrong with the notion of freedom it or something is wrong with the understanding of the notion of freedom. Perhaps absolute freedom cannot be freedom. Freedom in practice must accompany with restraints. Mutual freedom implies mutual regard for the other. Moreover, the unfolding of full story of freedom would also require an explication of the ideas such as reason, reasonableness and the concern for the other..

The idea of a *sanyasi* in the Hindu tradition seems to carry the notion of absolute freedom. A *sanyasi* is not supposed to stick to the ordinary rules and regulations which are applicable to a householder. Yet this does not mean that a *sanyasi* can steal, hurt or kill. Thus even a sanyasi does not have absolute freedom. It is clear that a proper understanding of freedom is a sine qua non of having proper relationship between me and the other.

This brief discussion points about the need for understanding the nature of self and also the nature of the other with whom one has to live in some way or the other. The fact of existence reveals the plurality of selves. If there is individuals more than one then they are bound to be different and distinct from each other. If they are different then they would feel, think, act and plan in different ways. This does not necessarily block a mutual, cooperative and harmonious relationship, provided egoism, narrow self-interest, undue expectations, exclusive and possessive tendencies are kept at bay. The 'other' may be a hell or a help, but it also depends, largely, on how the 'other' is perceived – as another 'I' or absolutely other.

Equality and Uniqueness

'To believe your own thought, to believe what is true for you in your private heart is true for all men – that is genius." Ralph Waldo Emerson

Looking at from the religious point of view, almost in every religion, it is preached that being the creation of the same Creator, all creatures are equal and thus brothers amongst themselves. However, two serious departures can be observed against this belief. First can be shown within the context of any religion itself and second is found in the prevalent inequality which is patent in all societies. In the religious context it is generally observed that followers of one religion do not view the followers of the other religion with amicability. Followers of the other religions are normally considered as being on wrong path and therefore as fallen beings. They have to be brought on the right path and if they persist in their wrong ways they should be either left to themselves or be shown out. They are not equal to the believers. In intent a religion is inclusive but in practice it is exclusive.

In spite of there being a religious institution in a society inequality in the status, inequality in rights, inequality in possessions, and inequality in treatment appear to be rampant all over. Inequality in terms of wealth and status has characterized societies in the world since times immemorial. In some cases even the wise men of the society failed to see its presence and consequent injustice done to a large section of society. Slavery was taken for granted in ancient Greek society in spite of there being the three great wise men – Socrates, Plato and Aristotle. A large section of society was considered as sudras in the Hindu society and this was not considered odd.

Though the idea of equality of beings was present since the ancient times, it came to be a propelling force many centuries later in socio-political context. It was during the tumultuous situations prevailed in the later eighteenth century France, known as French Revolution, that the three slogans – Liberty, Equality and Fraternity, acquired some substance. Later on the idea of a proletariat society as a part of communist doctrine became the inspiring source of socialist movement in Russia. These are well known facts of the history. While democratic systems prevail in most of the countries of the world to-day, as a consequence of these movements, inequality persists to vitiate social structure in various societies in various ways.

In the present context, I wish to emphasize the idea of equality as an inspiration and therefore as an ideal to consider all human beings on the same level. One is reminded here of the Kantian idea of the kingdom of ends (a society in which everybody would be treated as an end and not as means only). One of the ways in which Kant, the great German philosopher formulated his categorical imperative – a statement of duty, it meant that one should act in such a way that one treats the other person always as an end and never as a means only. That is, Kant had visualized a state of society in which every person was as worthy as any other and no one had to be treated as a means only. This principle blocks the possibility of exploitation of one individual by another.

Many people think that inequality is built in the society. It is preordained. There will always be some people who are rich and some people who are poor. That has been the rule since time immemorial. Those who believe in transmigration (a theory according to which there has been a life preceding the present one and there will be a life which will follow after this life is over), also believe that the differences based on inequality are found there because of the good or bad actions people did in their previous lives. In fact, one of the reasons to believe in the transmigration is the fact of uneven difference amongst people. However, the other opinion views the matter in an entirely different way. It is said, that the source of uneven differences is not to be found in previous lives but in the structure of the society itself and the structure of a society is a consequence of the thinking and doing of its members themselves. Since the structure as it obtains is arbitrary, it has to be changed. Once it is changed into a desirable design, uneven differences would go. This is the idea underlying the socialist and democratic views of the society.

Sometime a fact is adduced as a support for a certain policy or a principle. It may be said that all human beings are born as equal. That is, their status remains unaffected by social forms so far as the fact of their being born is concerned. Manu wrote that they are really born when they have passed through certain sacraments. Their physical birth remains immaterial till they attain a second birth (*dvija*) by going through the sacraments or *samskaras*. But the same author denied the right of having *samskaras* to a large section of the society, that is, to *sudras*. Thus this fact would not support the principle of equality in the proper sense. Similarly, when Rousseau declared that human beings in their natural state were free and it was society that put them under chain, he could be supposed to have indicated that in the natural state all human beings were equal. But both these positions do not indicate facts as such, but an opinionated view about a certain state of being of humans. Moreover, it is generally accepted that a principle of 'ought' cannot be derived from a given fact. If what is desirable already exists or prevails, then a command or advice that it ought to be brought about would not arise. A principle is a plea for launching an action in a certain way. The principle does not describe a given action. An action is an intervention into the state of affairs. In other words, it results into the change of a given state of affairs.

However, a fact is not irrelevant to the formation of a principle. In fact there is something which leads to an uneasiness in accepting a given state of affairs as it is. It is this uneasiness which induces a move towards changing or modifying the given state of affairs. Thus a principle comes to be formed as a rule for dealing with facts of a certain kind. There is something radically wrong with the structure of the society as it exists and that is why it becomes necessary to think about it and find ways to get rid of it. Inequality prevails in society in several ways. It militates against the very notion of a human being in terms of dignity and personhood and attempts are being made almost continually to get rid of it.

Thus equality can be treated as a regulative principle having for its source the fundamental recognition of human worth, to be applied to the policies and programs relating to change in a given structure of society. As has been well recognized, equality in this sense means that everyone should be treated before law in the same way, everyone is allowed to have opportunities for one's development and contributing to society equally, every human being is treated as an end. It would be a parody of the principle of equality to think that it is meant to produce clones of a certain type, that is, beings of the same type in certain given respects. One has to be aware of the dangers to which bio-technology might lead, if it is allowed to be used for a eugenics producing homogenous beings of a desired sort.

The principle of equality has to accommodate the idea of the uniqueness of every human being. It is only for certain sort of demands which are necessary for the growth of individuals and the well being of society that it is invoked and not for bringing all of them to the same size. The worth and dignity lies in the uniqueness of the individual. The character of 'standing out' has been well brought up by the German term *'dasein'* as used by Heidegger. In fact, the emphasis on the uniqueness of an individual was one of the main concerns of existentialist thinkers who brought about a radical change in thinking in the last mid - century. The idea was not entirely new. Earlier Nietzsche had talked of '*übermensch*' or superman. Man must surpass himself, said Nietzsche. Later Iqbal pleaded that man should raise himself to such heights that God Himself may ask him for his wish.

The transformative ideal has been the essence of philosophy of education. The second birth, that is, the notion of *dvija,* as Manu visualized, was a transformative concept. But what do we mean by the transformative concept. What is meant when it is demanded that man must surpass himself. Thinkers have been worried about this question and have tried to find an adequate answer since the earliest times. One of the earliest forms of this quest has been a search for the true or real nature or form of a human being. As is well known, many Indian thinkers identified this form as '*atma*' – self, soul or spirit. They conceived it as different from the body. No predicate that is applied to the body can be applied to '*atma*'. The real knowledge or right knowledge was conceived in terms of realization of this distinction of '*atma*' from the body.

To realize the distinction between body and *atma,* and to attempt a return to one's true or real form or nature that is as atma, has been conceived as the real transformative ideal. Such an attempt has been spelled out mainly in two distinct ways. To reach one's real form one must deny the illusory form. To reach atma one must deny body. But what does it mean to deny the body? Having body means having certain sort of cravings or desires. These cravings and desires are determined by our senses and sensations and affect most of our actions and behaviour. Most of the time most of us are busy in thinking and planning how to fulfill these cravings to their maximum. At times these cravings are so intense that they do not permit us to attend to their likely adverse consequences. They also make us utterly selfish. We hardly feel if there are others towards whom we have some duty. Any hurdle in the fulfillment of any of these desires drives us crazy. We get into a fury and our perception becomes blurred. We fail to see things as they are. As a consequence we just dash against a wall.

It is clear that according to one approach, most of our sorrows and pains are traced to the temptations of our body. The radical solution is that we get rid of our desires. Like the tortoise one should completely withdraw oneself from the objects of senses. (See *Gita*, 2-58). Only after such a withdrawal is it possible to move towards one's true self. Pushing the matter to its logical extreme would mean not only denial of the body but the extermination of the body. For so long one has the body one cannot completely free oneself from its cravings. It is interesting that this alternative was neither recommended nor was actually chosen by this tradition. Consequently less rigorous alternative came to be recommended. So long as one lived and one had to care for the body to the extent to which it was necessary to maintain life, what was necessary, was to minimize the desires and keep their fulfillment within limits. It was suggested that one should realize that the entire existence is pervaded by its master – *Isa*, one should not be greedy and should not yearn for somebody else's possessions. Maintaining such an attitude one should enjoy the world and may even wish to live for hundred years. (*Isopnisad*)

It is clear that whichever alternative one chose, realization of self as distinct from body and its cravings was an ideal purely individualistic and had little concern for the existence of other people or the society. Though, it would be wrong to think that it had absolutely no relationship with the sorrows or welfare of others in the society. A person who has learnt to live on the fulfillment of minimum needs and that too with a certain amount of self-control, could not cause harm to anyone and is likely to have greater concern and sympathy for the sufferings or the welfare of the other being less preoccupied with his own selfish ends. We have noted that part of the discipline of self-culture did point to the duty towards the other. It is also patent that very few people have a tendency to choose such a spiritual path. Since the notion of self-realization is not merely to realize one's true or real self but it also involves an identity with the being of beings (finding same *atma* or spirit in all the living beings) in the ultimate sense, such realized selves would be exceptional.

While the notion of *atma* does not permit within its content whatever can be associated with the body, it is devoid of such potentialities which could define the development of multiple aspects of personality. In fact, some of those who believed in the notion of *atma,* also believed that *atma* does not act. It's essential attribute is consciousness or *cit.* Which means it is a seer and not an actor. (Notice that this concept is diametrically opposed to the existentialist position according to which an individual is primarily an agent who makes choices and exercises freedom in actions). Views differing from this concept of *atma,* emphasize the acting part of self. So the central notion for them with regard to self is will. When the process of transformation of self is viewed from the point of potentialities and their development then again several approaches seems to have been adopted.

Often we hear of an all round development of personality as the ideal of education. However it is not very clear as to what is meant by 'all round development'. One of the possibilities may be that the child is as good in sports as in studies. In case this is considered insufficient then arts may be added to the list. Before we move further let's bring to our notice the quantum and variety of the possible areas of learning open to an aspirant in our times. On the one hand there is the realm of vast sciences and technologies and on the other there is the expanded realm of social sciences, medicine and management and humanities (which would include languages, literatures, and philosophies). Viewed in terms of the growingly specialized areas almost in each field the range of subjects becomes very large. Add to it various arts – music, painting, sculpture, dance and several others having in themselves immense range of varieties as determined by different cultures, and areas of several sports the variety of which can easily be visualized by going through the items included in Olympics and similar other global contests.

It should be clear that one cannot expect by the all rounded development, development of all these disciplines, and skills. Naturally this consideration renders the notion of all round development vague and contentious. Moreover, so far we have dealt with the content of what an aspirant possibly may be able to learn or acquire. We must also attend to certain dispositional attributes which enrich, strengthen the personality and make the individual more and better capable to interact with fellow beings and nature. An individual may have acquired lot of information in one or more fields but she or he may be incapable of handling it or applying it in a proper way. Such a state of affairs cannot define proper notion of education. Perhaps the notion of all round development may be better understood in terms of the development of desirable dispositional attributes in an individual.

It seems we are moving in the area of the development of individual's personality like an entrepreneur who is viewing the products to be turned out from her factory with certain designs and quality. The current phrase 'human resource' appears to be confined to something which can be manipulated, used or augmented for some non-human purpose. Obviously, something is radically wrong with our thinking in the present context, that is, the context of learning, education, and personality.

Every individual is different from the other in some essential respect/s. Each may have potentials – some are common with others, while some may be specific to the individual as distinguishing her or him from the other.

These potentialities may have genetic source or/and may have their source in the environment within which the individual exists and grows. Educationists have come to recognize that it is wrong to impose external choices as determining the course of educational development of the child. The correct thing would be that the potentialities and the interests of the child are identified and then they are given the facilities and proper environment so that the child develops according to its interests and potentialities. Such a course depends on the recognition of the uniqueness of each individual. The notion of equality would require that no child is deprived of the right to grow and develop and that no child is deprived of the facilities which would enable her to develop her potentialities.

Even within the same field or area individuals are found to have developed their capabilities or skills in their individual ways. Think of two classical singers such as Pt. Bhimsenjoshi and Pt. Jasraj. Both are great masters of their art and yet when they present the same raga in a certain mode they do so in their individual ways. If this happens within the same field or area, how much more would it be the case in the areas which are different from each other? A culture or civilization is known or identified by such masters unique in their individual ways? Strangely, sometimes it is found that individuals unique in some field being masters in their field, have no attunement amongst themselves. They form and establish different groups or camps. Their followers in order to maintain their different identities exaggerate differences which unfortunately sometime grow into hostile relationship. Great men must not allow uniqueness to degenerate into eccentricity.

Long back, Plato thought that the proportion between the intellectual elite and the general masses is the same as is found in the mass of brain and the rest of the body. Obviously, this idea militates with democratic spirit. One of the implications of this view is that the nature of things is such, that the loci of excellence would always remain limited within the few; most people would remain at a lower level, perhaps because they do not have the capability to attain the excellence. This has not been proved to be true. In recent times, some folk artists have attained international repute. Before they were identified and brought to the public notice, people hardly knew about them. Plato himself made a comment in his classical text – *Republic,* that it is possible that the next generation may not resemble the earlier one in the related excellence. So the selection of a candidate for an appropriate station should not depend on parentage but on the intrinsic qualities of the person concerned. This means that it is possible that the potentiality for a certain excellence may exist in any individual. That is, any individual may rise to a given peak provided the potentiality is identified and proper conditions for its growth are fulfilled.

Every individual can be visualized as a locus of potentiality of some excellence or the other. Thus each individual is intrinsically unique in her or his individual way. As already noted, when biographies of great individuals are written and published it is often found that these great men had a very non-distinctive childhood or even their later years to a point, had no pointer to greatness. If one were to consider the life span of Mohandas Karamchand Gandhi till the moment he was thrown out of the railway carriage at the Moritzberg station, it would be difficult to guess the rest of the events which raised him to the greatest heights. When we read about the childhood of Einstein, nothing seems to indicate the future career of one of the greatest scientist. These considerations seem to indicate that the factors which constitute the transformative process relating to an individual cannot perhaps be laid down in any systematic or comprehensive manner.

Yet the belief that schools, colleges and universities have to be there in any civilized society so that children and youths get the opportunity to educate themselves and to have their potential excellence developed, seems to be based on the hope that it is possible to determine the conditions which may help transform individuals into beings having some excellence or the other. The fact that our educational institutions have had limited success in their main objective on the one hand and the fact that certain individuals had attained excellence in spite of these institutions, raise doubts about external efforts to develop excellence.

It may, however, be noted that the fault does not lie in the understanding that the growth of excellence needs proper conditions, which the educational institutions may be able to provide, but the actual functioning of the so-called educational institutions. In our country alone, this question has been bothering all serious and thoughtful people. As a consequence several commissions were appointed in succession to investigate into the actual functioning of these institutions, and what can be done to make them better. We are all aware of the reasons why the recommendations of these commissions have had only very limited success in actual practice.

This would remain a persistent effort against various kinds of odds. Such an effort itself has for its source the élan vital which would continuously inform the quest for excellence. The point which needs to be emphasized is that the contradiction between democratic leveling and the right of each individual to develop his excellence in a unique way as being different from all others, is only apparent. We began by considering the notion of equality and it is clear that the democratic structure of society is based on the notion of equality. The main requirement of the notion of equality, as we understand it, is that every person is treated as an end and not as a means only. The personhood of each person must be recognized. This recognition entails several fundamental rights which form the preamble of Indian Constitution.

The condition of equality does not require that everybody is identified as having the same sort of potentialities, or that everybody should think alike or behave alike. Equality does not mean uniformity or homogeneity. Thus the notion of \ equality does not interfere with the notion of uniqueness. But we must remind ourselves that uniqueness does not admit the notion of very important person. The notion of VIP has vitiated our social frame. Neither there is a justification for such a privileged status of a person whatever position she or he occupies nor there is any justification for any privilege on that account. Unfortunately the prevalence of both these features is a glaring fact of our social and political life. They are however absolutely incompatible with the notion of justice on the one hand and the idea of the unique individuality having some excellence on the other.

The uniqueness of the individual lies in the freedom of choice and decision on the one hand and the inalienable position on the other. Each individual is so placed in a network that the view open to one would be different from the view open to the other. Thus the perspective open to one individual is different from the perspective open to the other. Besides each individual carries a store of psychic input which differs from that of the other in a unique way. The perspective and the psychic input determine to a large extent the way one looks at the world.

While it is true to say that each individual has the freedom of choice and decision, this is also true that the exercise of freedom does not take place in a vacuum, there are alternatives to choose from and there are considerations which determine the choice. Besides, an action requires the fulfillment of several conditions to make it possible. The issue relating to freedom and determinism must be viewed within this perspective. It may often be the case that external constraint or force seems to nullify the freedom of choice or decision. What happens is that individual does make a choice and takes a decision, though it may not be the one he would have preferred in different conditions.

Recent advances in bio-technology, in genomics have unfolded the possibilities of great interventions into the formation of nature and growth of an individual. They are remedial, formative as well as instrumental to designs. While the first two provide directions which may ameliorate the physical conditions of human growth, the third has potential dangers, in case the designs were to serve narrow ends of certain individuals. These advances also allow a possibility of having individuals all of the same sort or kind. Such a development can be compared to the uniform products of a factory. If such a possibility comes about to be actualized, the shape of the society would be poor and immensely boring. It would be leveling of human beings in the true sense and would do away with the uniqueness of an individual. Loss of one individual would be no more lamentable for there would be another of the same sort. Even if the whole lot is destroyed, there would be enough resources to develop such a lot again.

An understanding of nature and its processes, and the values mankind has discovered and nurtured so far and which make the planet worth livable, would in all probability, prevent such an eventuality to come about. The world would be richer because of multiplicity and variety of all sorts of unique human beings.

Man and Woman

"I would rather trust a woman's instinct than a man's reason.' Stanley Baldwin.

"A man does what he can; a woman does what a man cannot." Isabel Allende.

Life depends on both the principles – male and female. One is no more important or worthy than the other. But the story is much more complicated and provocative. In the patriarchal society generally, women have been considered subordinate to men and had to remain under the protection of men. The relationship between men and women can be considered from several points of view-descriptive and normative, psychological and individualistic, biological and historical, social and metaphysical. Since all societies are structured in terms of classes – professional, economic, and social, a uniform and clear picture of the relationship of man and woman cannot be described.

Historically speaking, major changes in the position of women have begun gradually emerging only in the twentieth century. The significant change can be indicated by the self – awareness of women which has been emerging collectively. Yet the majority of women are still bound with the age old restraints and restrictions. The source of these restraints and restrictions can be found in male chauvinism, women trying to live conforming to the image imposed on them by the males, the feeling of frailty and vulnerability in women themselves as infused in them by domestic training, dependence for the food and shelter on men, chastity and purity of women in order to maintain and sustain the property rights within the family, and the need for maintaining the household and the children. Some of these restraints and restrictions are - women will not move out independently, they will not befriend with male members other than those belonging to the family, they would be loyal to their husbands and obey and serve them, they would not think of their own interests or development at the cost of the functions in the family.

From the earliest times, women remained mainly confined to home, keeping and maintaining the home, preparing food, begetting children and looking after them. Men were supposed to move out and find resources for the home in terms of food, clothes and other necessities. Women could feel secure within the four walls while men would face all kinds of challenges which they were likely to meet once they went in search for food. This may be no exaggeration to say that the relationship between man and woman passes through the whole spectrum of emotions, depending on the temperament of each of them and the kind of conventions they consciously follow. In spite of the fact that conventionally a woman has to remain in loyal subordination to her husband, it may so happen that temperamentally she may turn out to be more dominant and it may also happen that the husband in spite of being physically strong may remain meek when facing his wife. They may fight with each other, may abuse each other and yet may not be able to break the relationship, though, that too is not an impossible happening.

If we go back in time in order to learn about how women and the relationship between them and men were visualized in the various traditions, we have for our sources mostly the writings of men folk. So far as the sacred texts are concerned, their content is normally attributed to revelation and extra-human origin. But they have been scribed, collected and edited only by the male members of the community. One can imagine, how the injunctions about women would proceed if these texts were scribed by the males. Yet there are texts which belie such suspicions. From *Vaidik samhitas*, we learn about the lady-*rishies* – *rishikas*, three goddesses, and women of independent temper such as Lopa Mudra. Later in Upanisads we learn of Maitreyi and Gargi – two ladies well versed in higher learning. In *Mahabharata*, an inquisitive aspirant was sent to a household lady to attain wisdom. In Christianity, Mary and in Islam Khadija, Aisha and Fatima are held in great respect. Khadija was a lady running a business and having been convinced of the character and efficiency of her manager, that is Muhammad, married him. Perhaps such examples can be found elsewhere also, but they are rather exceptions and serve as showcases rather than the rule.

It would be interesting and instructive to go further in the Hindu context, for here we meet the whole range of attitudes towards women – from a *dasi* (a maid servant) to a *devi* (a godess). Almost every major god has a consort. In most temples the divine images consist both of the god as well as the goddess. There are temples where only the male god is established, similarly there are also temples where only goddess is worshipped. It is interesting to note that the divine source of wisdom, knowledge and arts is goddess Saraswati, but when we talk of *upanayana samskara* is talked about there is mention of boys but not of girls. There is a mention of great learned women, but no girl student is listed while a *gurukula* is described. It is well known that when Mandan Misra had accepted defeat in the arguments with Sankaracarya, wife of Misra argued that unless Sankara defeats her also in the *sastrartha*, the defeat would be taken as incomplete. The debates between Maitreyi and Yajnyavalkya, and Gargi and Yajnyavalkya are famous. It is said that where women are respected blessings of gods are present, but at the same time it is also recommended that women should remain under the protection of some male member, - father, husband and then the son. Women were considered temptations for the great *rsies*. Stories of Indra being afraid of a *rsi* performing penances or *tapas* and trying to spoil his *tapas* by persuading *apsaras* to tempt him, are many. Yet women are worshipped as goddesses as Sakti and Durga. Mother is held in reverence as greater than both teacher and father, yet a woman has generally been considered as subordinate to male. There is frequent mention of *daises* accompanying the bride when she departs for her new home.

One may try to get rid of the inconsistencies evident in the above description by contextualizing the episodes, yet it seems that men folk have generally found themselves as weak against women and it is because of this basic scare that ambivalent attitudes towards women have come to be developed. This can be said for males irrespective of the culture to which they belong. The inferiority complex generally manifests itself in the show and exercise of superiority. The complex emerges from the lack of self-control while an encounter with the opposite sex takes place. That is why women are considered as snares and temptations for sin. A little less derogatory image indicates the role of women as objects. In the well known school of Indian thinking – samkhya, *prakrti* is compared with a dancer. When her dance comes to an end *purusa* retires. Of course, this image is merely a metaphor meant to explain a certain abstract metaphysical point, yet it indicates the generally held belief about women in the male mind.

The crucial story relating to male and female relationship begins at the level of asymmetric position between the two. Each is likely to treat the other as an object. An object is something to be possessed, consumed, enjoyed or exploited. Such an asymmetric relation obtains not only amongst the opposite sexes but also between any two persons irrespective of gender. The morbid nature of such a relationship cannot be overstated. Pick up any newspaper of any day and some episodes of heinous crimes as a result of such a morbid relationship would be there. The rise of feminist movement during the last century arose as a consequence of prevalence of the said asymmetric relationship. Basically the movement remained confined to female elites, as females at the lowest rung were hardly aware of it though they were the greatest sufferers.

The story of Sojourner Truth, an American slave woman, initially sold at many hands, and later became a free woman (when the slavery was abolished), rose to the occasion and spoke for her rights as the rights of white women is one of the earliest known episodes in the history of feminism. The story can be found in the Wikipedia under the caption 'Sojourner Truth'. The crucial issue involved in the feministic debate has to do with a fundamental distinction which is built upon the natural or biological difference between man and woman and on which depend the arguments for and against the symmetry or asymmetry between man and woman.

No one can deny the biological difference between man and woman. But what can be made out of it. Do women have less physical energy or force as compared to men, are they incapable of performing certain physical feats which only men can do, do they have less intelligence or capacity to think as compared to men, can they fight like men, is their imaginative power inferior to men in that that they cannot be great artists or litterateurs, do they have less endurance then men in performing stressful tasks – these are the various questions which arise when the physical strength of women is compared with that of men. The desire or idea to prevent women from entering into certain areas traditionally considered as male bastions, tend to answer these questions in affirmative. But the fact of the matter is, that almost in all these areas, women have shown that these questions can be answered in the negative. They have proved themselves as pilots, as soldiers, as commandos, as athletes, drivers, engineers, architects, artists, litterateurs and have also proved their ability in many hazardous occupations. In fact it is not so much the matter relating to physical differences between male and female but it is a question relating to the state of mind concerning power, control and ownership.

Several other stereotypes came to be associated with women. They cannot be relied upon. No secrets should be committed to them. They cannot be reliable witnesses. They are soft and emotional. They cannot control themselves. They cannot perform highly intellectual exercises. One cannot rely on them for serious and grave decisions. The list can be prolonged. Every one of these has been disproved. There is no important or high office which requires high intellectual capabilities women do not possess. In some cases they have held these offices for a quite a long time.

In terms of disposition certain characteristics are associated with masculinity, while certain other characteristics are associated with femininity. Valour, courage, confidence, endurance, adventure and dominant temper are generally associated with masculinity and tenderness, tolerance, caring, meekness, and submissiveness are supposed to be characteristic of women. Men are supposed to rely more on intellect, while women seem to be inclined to rely on feeling or intuition. Generally such a distinction seems to have some plausibility. But numerous examples can be cited which would not support such a distinction. One thing should be kept in mind and that is differential bearing and nurturing of the sons and daughters. Daughters are often brought up with an awareness of being weaker sex. They are required to be modest, less talkative, and shy. They are generally advised not to take hard physical tasks which are basically meant for the boys. They are generally not allowed to venture to move out without a consort.

In contrast boys are required to be tough, confident and venturesome. They are not prevented from moving out alone and are supposed to perform various errands outside home. Girls are confined to kitchen, and are supposed to learn sewing, knitting, even some music, while boys are supposed to be skilled in physical feats, sports and the like. One can find the boys of a locality going out for sporting some game like cricket or foot-ball. But generally it is not found that the girls of the locality would collect together and go out for similar sports.

We seem to be living in a stage of transition. There is lot of discussion and debates going on about how the children should be brought up. Particularly the attention of the parents is being drawn to the fact that they should not bring up their children with gender discrimination. The idea is gradually and slowly seeping in the minds of parents, though still in a small percentage. We find now girls achieving high scores in all those fields which were mainly dominated by the boys. Very recently a woman from a dalit family of Kaithal (a small place in Rajasthan), succeeded in climbing Everest. And who does not know the well known ex-police officer Kiran Bedi, who has proved that some time women can do better in the jobs formerly supposed to be done only by the males. Think of Margaret Thatcher, Indra Gandhi, who had the rein of their countries in their hands. Angela Merkel, Chancellor of Germany has been recently said to be second most powerful personality in the world of politics.

The cultural aspect of child bearing and nurturing is extremely significant. Culture, of course, is determined by the beliefs and practices that people follow collectively over a long period of time. The needs of life and a reliable and facilitating social set up lead to the selection of beliefs and practices which support life and society. But things keep on changing with new needs, knowledge and understanding, and new happenings and encounters. The beliefs and practices of a people also change though extremely slowly. The tension between the reliance on the old and need of the present generates conflicting problems for any society. Introduction of new inventions and gadgets during the course of last few decades have brought about radical changes in the life style of people all over the world. The means of travel and communication are getting fast and faster and gradually reaching a large population. What happens in one part of the globe comes to be known in another part of the globe almost simultaneously. Such changes stir the beliefs held for ages and new necessities make it imperative to change our ways of living.

While the encounter between people of different cultures has resulted in the greater understanding of each other, it has also generated a quite different kind of movement, which in a sense, has an opposite and even an unhappy impact. The 'other' has led me to a more intense self conscious 'I'. In order to differentiate from the other I have suddenly become more conscious of my self-identity. The question is how to spell out my identity; how I am to understand that I am different from the other. I naturally fall back on my own habitat, tradition and culture. But do I understand, do I know what the culture or tradition is, to which I belong? I make some ad hoc adjustments and pick up beliefs and practices which are prevalent to distinguish my life-style. I am not very sure if I really understand these beliefs and practices. I accept them just because they are there and my elders have been following them. I do not bother to go to the roots. I do not suspect if they are really relevant. On top of it I think, what I follow is the best way I have chosen and what does not match with it must be rejected, or at least not be considered worthy of respect. That is what can be said about most of us.

Such a quest of identity and its maintenance involves an abhorrence of the other and this is something dangerous. Unreflective and uncritical attachment to identity manifests itself sometime in very inhuman ways. Recent honour killings in Haryana (a state in India) and the judgments of khap panchayatas (the village judiciary organizations) and elsewhere also illustrate the cruel attitude. Such a thing is also evident from the beliefs and violent practices of talibani muslims. On the other hand moderates in the Muslim community have started insisting to have science oriented education for their children – both boys and girls. Women are being appointed on senior and important positions even in Vatican, which was sometime back wholly a male domain.

Coming back to the relationship between man and woman, the awareness of mutual regard and concern is replacing the old traditional belief that women are subordinate to men and major decisions rest with males. As already noted, in Indian tradition while there is a strong stream which holds women very high in esteem, yet in practice they have not been treated well. One very important factor responsible for such an asymmetry can be found in the acceptance of the image which males have imposed on the feminine consciousness.

This fact can be generalized in respect of women in general. Women look at themselves as objects for men. Mutual relations amongst women themselves are also often determined in the context of male gaze or appreciation. This has led to conspiracies, cruelties, and ill treatment of women by women themselves. On the other hand men have found themselves, as already noted, weak when it comes to their relation with women as they become easy prey to their enticement. But things are not as simple as that. Men have also considered women just playthings for their pleasure. A large amount of literary fiction would attest to these complexities. Literature, as is often said, mirrors state of affairs in the society.

Such an unhappy situation obtains, basically because of one reason and that is the absence of mutual regard and concern. This is true as much of the relation between man and woman as it is amongst the men folk themselves.

The rise of the feminist movement during the last century was a consequence of the prevailing asymmetry and gender roles and relationships. As is well known the initial agenda began with the goal of emancipation from the male domination. This however, soon morphed into attempts to appropriate the male identity in the sense that women were equal to men because they can live just like men. And finally the insight dawned that the most appropriate relationship consists in complementariness between male and female. Thus the movement seems to have had three phases with three different goals – freedom from men; equality with men; and equality with men affirming the intrinsic difference from them.

So far we have been considering the relation between men and women as if such a relationship has nothing do with children or family. Of course, there are any numbers of contexts in society in which men and women are likely to encounter each other outside the family ties. But most members of society are tied in the family relationships. In fact, family can be seen as a link between nature and society. Natural processes involve continuity of species. Family provides a systematic rule governed frame for human propogation. From the Indian point of view the first issue out of wedlock was called '*dharmaja*'. The later issues were called '*kamaja*'. While one can read the first indication of family planning in such a perspective, it may have different interpretations also. For example, it may have been just a descriptive explanation of the sequence of child births.

It is important to realize the importance of the family frame in view of the growing permissiveness in the man and woman relationship. The unscrupulous, irresponsible, and inquisitive advances of males, the unbridled desire of freedom, emotional tides, absence of the awareness of remote consequences, lack of mutual and mature understanding generally push teens into relationships which they later repent if at all. This is a global phenomenon and what is most worrying in such relationships is the possibility of development of indifferent and callous attitudes to one another in other spheres of life also. If pleasure comes to dominate and person recedes into background, then humanity would be reduced to inert objects. Love, compassion, friendship, loyalty and respect would become historical curios.

Child brings human touch to the loving relationship between man and woman. And this seems crucial for the family frame. Family is an economic and social unit. It is a repository and a carrier of culture and tradition which are distinctive of a society. It is here that the child finds itself amongst other human beings. The first human being it comes in contact with is its mother. Mother is the loving, protective and guiding force for the child throughout its life. The loving care of the parents provides the child all the initial support and the facilities which would gradually transform it into a confident and independent being who can find her or his way into the world and even create her or his own paths. It is in the family frame, that the human being first acquires the basic sense of values, learns to live with other human beings, finds opportunities to get skills, and acquires knowledge necessary for survival and to qualify her or him for being a member of the society. The child thus has a dual relationship in the family. Being the centre of the family it brings the members of the family, specially the parents close to each other and it owes its induction into the world to the care and love of the family members.

This description of family is brief and it ignores the fact that family exists and has existed in various modes and forms –joint and nuclear, matrilocal and patrilocal, matriarchal and patriarchal, monogamous or polygamous and so on. The modes of the family would also differ according to its place in the society. A society is generally divided into various segments according to economic and cultural divisions. For instance, in our country, the caste distinctions and hierarchies divide the society into numerous segments. The mode and the form of the family would differ from each other according to which rung it belongs to. Another important feature to keep in mind is the fact of social mobility which is determined by the economic and social development. Social mobility itself brings about changes in the mode of the family pattern. While the basics remain same or similar, the inter-relationship amongst the members, the modes of child care, the shape of projects are likely to undergo changes according to the status a family occupies in the society.

Diverse occupational demands that often divide family members constitute yet another factor in determining the forms of various family units. In some cases the father has to work in some far away place, and the burden of the family maintenance falls back either on the older people or the mother. In some cases father and mother work at different places. In many cases permanent stay at one place is not possible because of the transfers involved in the jobs. Naturally these factors have their impact on the bringing up of children. Notwithstanding these factors, the very idea of child's welfare, its growth and development remain the cementing force which keeps a family intact. Naturally it also determines the relationship between husband and wife, man and woman.

We also hear of the possible break down of the family structure. Socially, family structure was disrupted in the early stages of changes brought about by communist revolution both in Russia and China. That had an adverse effect on the values both in relation to family and society. In order to avoid the possible danger to the social fabric itself, the family structure became once again important. Another source likely to affect the family structure adversely seems to lie in the unbridled idea of freedom restricted to one's own convenience and pleasure on the one hand and the advances being made in bio-technology.

We are reminded of the chemical laboratory as described in the thought provoking fiction entitled *The Brave New World* by Aldous Huxley, written several decades ago, in which children would be hatched chemically and would be allowed to grow in the laboratory conditions. There are several important aspects relating to such an idea, but the most radical idea is dispensing with the idea of parent-hood. This of course would lead to the total disappearance of family frame. The recent success achieved in synthesizing bacterial life in the laboratory may one day result into the chemical laboratory of brave new world, if attempts are not made to regulate and control the sequence of events as implied in the said success.

This mechanical and technical move in scientific research seems to ignore the basic emotional demands inbuilt in the human existence responsible for the coherence and harmony amongst mankind. Reason as devoid of emotion or emotion devoid of reason would be inimical to the essence of humanness. (Think of the controversy between the way Plato and Rousseau looked at the relation between reason and emotion in the context of family.) A development which ignores this basic truth would lead mankind to the verge of its extinction. Let me be clear. I am not suggesting the synonymy between man and reason or emotion and woman. We are told by the psychologists that the mix of reason and emotion belongs to every human being irrespective of gender. Thus it is important to keep off this distinction between reason and emotion as between man and woman for herein lie the origin of an artificial as well as prejudicial gender division.

From the brief discussion about the relationship between man and woman above, we arrive at the conclusion that an ideal of a worthy and happy world remain a vain objective unless a mutual and loving concern and respect for each other amongst human beings in general and in man and woman in particular does not become an actuality.

Love and Hate

*"Without contraries (there) is no progression.
Attraction and repulsion, reason and energy,
love and hate, are necessary to human existence."*
William Blake

It is generally said that pain and pleasure are the two masters that regulate and control the thinking and behavior of all human beings. This may be an issue of debate, but few would disagree with the proposition that love and hate are two most powerful emotions which bring human beings closer to each other or push them apart. Since they operate on the relations of human beings, it is clear how important they are in respect of the cohesion or shattering of a society.

Emotions do not operate in an independent manner. There are several other factors relating to human behavior with which emotions come to be attached. Our needs and wants, interests and projects, our understanding of how things happen, and our beliefs about our fellow beings, the experiences and the learning from past which we have gained consciously or unconsciously, formally or informally and the world in which we live – all these go to weave the web of our thinking, inform our attitude and consequently determine how we act and how we form and see our mutual relationships.

While cognition relates to 'what' of things and happenings, and 'whom' in respect of individuals, our affective side seems to do with bonding or dissociating with them. Some feelings are always associated with such relationship. Sometimes, we may be completely indifferent or may have zero level of feelings, but the fact seems to be that feeling dimension is never absent completely from our consciousness. Feelings in the form of emotions exhibit the various ways in which we react to the world.

It is interesting to note that emotions in both the forms – negative and positive, play a very important role in our experience as well as in our personality make up. They may relate to the state of our body, it may be in a comfortable state or it may be in some sort of uneasy state; and they may relate to social context, in which others besides the individual are involved.

We are told to hate evil, injustice, and indignity on the one hand, but to love our neighbour, act with dignity and be honest and just. We must learn what to like and prefer, and what to dislike and give up. If emotional learning gets distorted in the sense that we start liking what we should not like and dislike what we what we should like, then we are likely to develop sick personality on the one hand and a hostile world around us on the other.

The crucial question that would arise here is what would determine what one should like and what one should not like. What would be the criteria of likeable and its opposite, preferable or not preferable, or desirable or undesirable? Can we have the same identical criteria as applicable to anything and everything without discrimination? And can this position be held in respect of every culture?

The question relating to 'should' can be deferred for the moment. Let us ask what people actually like or dislike. It is obvious that the answer would differ from individual to individual and also require attention to culture to which an individual belongs. Most likes or dislikes are acquired in one's childhood. Children pick up what goes around them. The kind of food that they are served, the clothes that they are made to wear, the language and mannerisms which they acquire by what they hear and see, remain with them throughout the later part of their lives. As they grow and their self-consciousness develops they may start having ideas as to what to prefer or like and give up what they learnt to dislike, consciously or unconsciously. The impact of their surroundings and the company they keep seep into their personality mostly without their knowing. Most of us do not know how and when we acquired certain like or dislike.

Likes and dislikes would not matter much, if they had no effect on or relationship with what we think and how we act. Our thoughts, beliefs, attitude and behaviour have their impact on the other people. Suppose, as a child I was served non-vegetarian food and I started to like it. I would hardly ever think whether I should continue with such food or give it up. I might not ever think that there could be something wrong with it. In fact, I may feel surprised when I find that there are people who do not like non-vegetarian food. It would be still more difficult to understand if I find people who are vegetarian and who have some sort of aversion to non-vegetarian food, even towards people who are non-vegetarians. When issues like cow-slaughter would come up, it becomes difficult for a person like me (but let me tell you, I am, in fact, a pure vegetarian) to understand what the halla balu is about, while for the vegetarians it is clear and obvious that cow-slaughter is a heinous practice and must be given up at the earliest. Of course, the religious component in the debate makes the matter worse.

This becomes clear when it is realized that in cultures in which non-vegetarianism is a routine matter, the animal to be killed for such a food becomes a bone of contention within the non-vegetarians themselves.

Living with certain beliefs and habits right from our childhood has its effect on a whole range of custom and practices which come to define our cultural profile. Apart from food, think of the kind of utensils used, the manner of cooking the food, the manner of serving or enjoying our food, the types of clothes we wear, the style of hair or beard that we maintain, the way we build our houses, the family relationships with members other than parents, the way marriage is understood and the various customs and rituals that people observe in its performance, the mode of behaviour which it is thought children should learn, and the religious beliefs and practices which are observed in a family.

Quite a big part of what an individual learns and acquires as a member of a family and thereby being a member of a segment of society, assumes a rigid attitude, in a comparative measure, if the society of which the individual is a member is a closed society like a tribal society or even a rural society. Even when such an individual shifts to an urban configuration, he or she carries with him or her, the rigid attitude already formed during his or her growth. The likes and dislikes and consequently the appreciation and evaluation are to a large extent determined by the already formed attitude, beliefs and habits. Since the individual is hardly aware as to how the attitude, beliefs and habits have come to be formed, the individual takes them to be quite natural and beyond any doubt.

When confronted with people belonging to a different society or segment of society one finds the ways and manners of the other people strange, unnatural even ridiculous. The realization that there are other societies different from the one to which the individual belongs, and that there are different ways and manners in which other people live, gradually softens the feelings of strangeness. Even then one hardly ever thinks to pick up or adopt any of those strange manners. Generally they are looked down upon and one condescends to adjust with others.

In fact confrontation with others need not result in some definite kind of reaction or response.

While there may be many possibilities, at least two of them stand out quite clearly. In one case an encounter forces a reflection on one's beliefs and way of life. One sometimes starts entertaining doubts about the rationality of some beliefs or some practices which one had taken to be right and natural so far and one's attention may be forced to consider the rationality of the ways of living of other people. In contrast, in the other case, the individual may become still more convinced of the naturalness and rightness of one's own beliefs and practices when compared with those of others. Such a thing happens, when the individual becomes worried about one's identity which also involves the feeling of superiority. Any kind of compromise in the relationship appears to endanger security and solidarity.

It is interesting to note that there are right kind of ideas and right kind of practices which seem to have an intrinsic attraction for an unbiased and unmotivated consciousness. For example a friendly smile, kind disposition, helping attitude, accommodating approach, and recognizing regard are generally appreciated anywhere in the world. The condition of being unbiased or unmotivated is important. In the absence of such a condition, and in a sick disposition even these gestures may become suspicious or be seen as ill motivated.

An encounter between any two individuals would be an encounter between two histories fed by a certain amount of input acquired formally or informally, consciously or unconsciously. Each of these two persons would thus have a distinctive mental disposition. It is obvious that each of these persons would act or react according to the mental make up that one has. It is very likely, therefore, that the two individuals having two different dispositions or two mental sets will have their own specific way to view the world and what goes on in it.

It is further clear that the view of the world would also be determined by the position one has in space and time. One looks at the world from where one is in the spacio-temporal frame. The one, who holds the camera, does not appear in the photograph one shots. Moreover, a photograph would change according to the change of the position of the photographer. This consideration recommends that one should try to visualize things from different positions, in order to have a better and many-sided picture. This is particularly true in respect of people other than me when I think or view them. I must attempt to place myself in the position of the other person as far as that is possible before making any judgment about what the other person says or does. This is easier said then done. My own preoccupations, projects, already held images about others interfere with my attempt to empathize. It is obvious that this much may as well be true so far as the other person is also concerned. S/he may also regard me with something on her/his back of mind consciously or unconsciously.

All these considerations weave and colour my likes and dislikes. I hate or love because I had some sort of experiences. I hate and love because I have learnt to like or dislike things. I seldom assess my feelings in an unbiased or critical way. Thus what I think about the world, other persons and things and the manner in which I approach any of them, is determined by considerations described above.

There is one more and important consideration which has a tremendous impact on my affective life. This consideration requires a spelling out the possessive 'my' or 'mine'. My body, my ideas, my family, my language, my school, my friends, my town, my state and my country, my culture and my traditions, these possessions which seem to make me what I am, which give me an identity, which distinguish me from all others, also tend to determine what I like or dislike. Attachment to my possessions is most of the time uncritical. My occupations leave little time for me to think about them or to evaluate them. Mostly I stick to them just because they are mine or I belong to them. A feeling of superiority embeds my concern with all that is mine.

In a way there is nothing wrong in having such an attachment. In fact what passes by the name of education is often oriented towards reinforcing this attachment. Such an attachment is supposed to enhance the feeling of pride and thereby confidence and give strength to maintain and sustain one's heritage and save it from the onslaught of the enemy. Unfortunately it is accompanied by the feeling of indifference to, lack of appreciation for, and at worst with hyper-criticality with the ways of the others. We tend to ridicule and deride the way other people live or behave. Clearly such a situation allows misunderstandings to develop and hostilities to flourish.

It does not occur to us that it is an accident that we are born in one family and not the other, in one period of history and not the other, in one society and not the other, in one country and not the other. The situation could have been quite different if we belonged to people other than those to whom we belong at present. How funny it is that we live throughout with the cognitive and emotive baggage lent to us by the accident of birth. I can see a mischievous smile on the face of my adversary who may be condescending towards my naivety thinking that it is wrong to take one's birth as an accident. It is all pre-determined according to a cosmic plan. I am what I am not because of accidents but because of a whole chain of my previous births and my doings in those births. However, such a view belongs to a certain tradition of thinking and beliefs and differs from other traditions and this fact alone makes this questionable. Even if the idea of the chain of birth is accepted, it itself does not guarantee that a human being would get the body of a human being in the next birth, or a Hindu will be born in a Hindu family, or a person of a certain caste will have birth in the same caste in the other life. Thus the configuration of human beings would continue from birth to birth, if the idea of chain of birth is accepted. It is interesting to note that the theory of rebirth is not confined in its application to any particular location on the globe. That means that a person who dies in India may have her or his rebirth in China or any other country. The implication of this point would lead to certain positions which may not be in consonance with the social structure.

So far we were engaged in an attempt to understand what considerations determine our affective life and our likes or dislikes, our loves and hates. We know that our affective aspect of our living either binds us with others or separates us from them. It allows us to move in certain directions or it prevents us from moving in certain other directions. To some extent this determines our projects and plans and their forms. Thus if we allow ourselves to float in an unreflective or unconscious way we cannot be sure of the rightness of the direction in which we let ourselves be pushed.

This requires us to be self-reflective. But what does it mean to be self-reflective.? To be self-reflective is to be self-conscious. That is, I should be conscious of what I am thinking, what I am planning, what I propose to do. This much alone would not do. I should try to see why I am thinking what I am thinking, why I am planning what I am planning, why do I want to do what I want to do. That is I should look for reasons for what I think, plan or propose to do. How can I assure myself, that the reasons which I discover in this process are good reasons?

These reasons may be influenced by my likes or dislikes which already inform my disposition. That is, I may choose my reasons because they are backed by my likes or dislikes. Besides, the choice of reasons may also be influenced by how I see the world around me and as already explained, in this I may be influenced by what I have experienced in my encounter with the world.

What I do not realize in this, is the fact that I am also involved in the encounter. There is action and there is reaction and this is bipolar. It is quite likely that what I receive from the world is a reaction to what I do to the world. It is difficult to take notice of this because my gaze, in a natural way, is directed towards what is away from me and does not allow me to notice that I am also there. As already noticed, the photographer has his entire attention on the view she or he wants to shoot and has little awareness of the fact that her or his view is determined by her or his own position. Obviously, an effort would be needed to be aware of this fact. But once I realize this fact, I would be able to see that the experience I had as a consequence of the encounter with the world has been a result of a mutual impact.

Such an effort would make an essential component of my self-reflection. This may allow me to view my experience in a more objective and unbiased way. This would also enable me sort out good reasons from bad reasons. Bad reasons, may precede my intent or intention, or explain it in some way, but they remain irrelevant so far as the justification of my intention or act is concerned. The search for good reasons can be facilitated by the awareness of my position in a larger network of which I form a part and also by the awareness of future consequences for me and for others of my act.

In other words, when my vision is confined narrowly to my immediate gains or losses, and only to my gains and losses, or is blurred by the intensity of desire, pain or pleasure, I fail in my search for good reasons. To be conscious about what I do or plan to do, indicates one dimension of self-reflection. Another dimension of self-reflection may have to do with what I have done, that is, I may reflect on my past doings or past sufferings or achievements. My achievements do not pose a grave problem, on the other hand they may boost my confidence, but my failures or departures from right path may pose serious problems for me. I may become aware of having committed mistakes, or may have acted towards others in an undesirable way, or I may be guilty of having committed some crime or sin. I may develop a guilt-consciousness and that is likely to vitiate my thinking in such a way that I am unable to assess my present problems in right perspective. I may feel ashamed and my confidence may get shattered. This might adversely affect my relationship with others. I may develop certain defence- mechanism such as projecting my negative feelings on others. I may start looking at others with suspicion and may even become paranoiac. I may become suspicious of everyone and may start thinking that everyone is hatching a conspiracy against me.

Still more dangerous would be to have developed an attitude of justification for whatever wrongs I may have committed. I may start thinking that I am not the one who has deviated from the right path. There are others who commit all kinds of wrongs and enjoy their lives. In fact, this is a sad feeling which sometimes overcomes many of us when we find that right actions and good disposition result in sorrow and misery and wrong action and evil disposition earn for one all the pleasures of life. Such a feeling poses a serious problem and needs a separate treatment. In the present context this affords a reason, though a bad one, to go on following the wrong path with the hope that it would bring us wealth and prosperity. In fact, while following the wrong path we do not think that it is really a wrong path. We delude ourselves into thinking that clever people do not bother about moral scruples and are adept in taking advantage of the opportunities that come their way. Such an approach saves us from morbid depression but turns us into die-hard wrong doers.

Such follow ups of past require that we develop a positive, corrective and healthy approach to our past. I should realize that, being humans and finite beings, we are liable to make mistakes and fall into the error of taking wrong paths in place of the right ones. Instead of getting depressed and feeling guilty about my past mistakes and wrongs, I should feel better, in the sense that now I know that I did make mistakes and did act wrongly. Since I now know that certain acts were not right, the first thing that I should decide is to determine myself not to commit them again. It may be that I find myself in a situation in which it is difficult to extricate myself from the mire I got stuck in I need to take hard decision and be ready to pay the cost for my deviation. It is difficult but it seems to be the only way to be free from perpetuation of evil.

We began by considering the proposition that human beings are moved by love or hate. We like things or dislike them. We love some human beings and hate some human beings. We have noticed that our likes or dislikes, our love and hate are not spontaneous feelings but are determined by our past experience informed by conscious and unconscious impacts. These impacts may have been rational or otherwise. Even the notions of rational or irrational are not independent notions. They may be culture bound. In such a state of affairs an examination of what we think or do becomes imperative. Now the question is in what way our self-reflection can help us to rationally determine our likes or dislikes, our love or hate?

We just stated that likes or dislikes are not spontaneous. This may be disputed. Perhaps we need to distinguish spontaneous feelings from deliberate preferences or approvals. While we choose objects in a shop, we may just pick up some item with some particular colour, shape or size in the first instance. We may sometime start thinking about the utility, cost and other relevant considerations. This deliberation may modify our choice at a later stage. It is also possible that there is someone who accompanies us on such an occasion. It may be necessary to take into account the thought and choice of our companion. Thus our final choice may have several components as effective in our preference. Feeling alone may not be the basis of choice. It is possible that it may turn out to be a dominating factor. The point is that feeling is a separate component and is other than the consideration of utility, cost, et cetera.

Something similar seems to happen when one develops a liking for a person. This liking in an intense form may be the feeling of love. In such a case, it is generally said that someone has fallen in love with someone, or it may have been the case of falling in love at first sight. It is also well known, that it is difficult to differentiate such a feeling from infatuation or lust. It may be momentary, it may persist, it may be natural or it may be an abnormal impulse. The resulting ties have been seen to last or terminate after a while. To what extent would it be possible to hold that such feelings are purely spontaneous and are completely independent from the influences of one's bringing up? Could such a thing happen between a person of one race and a person of another race – say between a European and an African? Perhaps, no more can be said with certainty except that it is less likely between the two persons of different races or cultures, than between the persons belonging to the same race or culture. A generalization can be hazardous. To the extent to which such a happening is determined by the cultural component, it could be inferred that it is not completely spontaneous.

Perhaps, it may be more reasonable to hold that the total make up of a person at a given moment may be at the back of the feeling of love at first sight. The make up being at the back is obviously not in the cognitive field and the incident may be attributed to feeling alone. Another important point to note is that it is not at all necessary that the attraction is mutual. In that case it would not be right to call it love if love is considered something mutual. All these considerations would render the case of falling in love at the first sight as a problematic event.

Another significant point to notice is the effect of the practice to think of the various mental faculties as being independent from each other. For long it has been thought that functions such as feeling, imagination, intuition, sensations, intellect, will and so on are separate and associated with the independent faculties of the mind. While it is true that some one of these may be more dominating, generally all our experiences – cognitive, aesthetic, moral or even spiritual, have all these components contributing their bits to the whole we call experience. If this is granted, then the talk of pure feeling would loose its plausibility.

If feelings are not independent, they are active in the total orchestra of experience, critical deliberation may be said to have an important role in determining their direction. If this be granted, then the idea of bringing in 'should' in our emotional make up acquires some importance. One can meaningfully hold that emotions have educative force, they need be trained to be associated with discrimination, so as to enable one to choose what one should and what one should not hate or love.

Assuming that hate and love are not spontaneous, that they can form important components of educative process; children can be taught what they ought to hate and what they ought to love. To begin with hygienic training involves inculcating a sense of cleanliness and avoiding dirty things and habits. They are served certain kind of food which they start liking. They are told not speak a lie, not to steal, not to hurt their siblings or companions, and to respect their elders. Technical gadgets are gradually becoming part of every household. Television, DVD players, computers, mobiles are becoming necessary part of domestic furniture. Children quickly acquire expertise in handling them and start using them for their pleasure. All kinds of inputs are available on these electronic sources – some of them are suitable for the consumption of children while some of them need to be avoided. It is a difficult exercise for the parents to persuade their children what things to like and watch and what they should avoid.

Children are also taught how they ought to behave with their neighbours. Actual practice in these areas may not be consonant with how things ought to be. Much depends how elders look on these matters. The class of society to which they belong also determines their attitude, deportment and way of life. This, naturally, percolates in the attitudes and deportment of their children. Children can be told to speak truth and to love justice. But this requires that they know what is 'truth' and what is 'justice'. If children find servants in the household being treated as unequals, being not given any respect due to human beings, and being indifferent to their fatigue and sickness, they are likely to take such behaviour as natural and there being nothing wrong in it. For them there would be nothing like unjust in such a behavior. If white children are told not to associate with the black ones, or Hindu children are not to associate with Muslim or Christian ones or vice versa, they are likely to take all these as part of life and may carry over such discriminatory behaviour in their later life. Their hates and loves would be informed accordingly.

Unless the undesirable discriminatory components in the attitude and deportment of the elders are shed, proper educative process would remain a mirage. Discrimination has to shift from the classes of human beings to beliefs, habits and ways of living. The significance of continual self- reflection in respect of the beliefs, habits and ways of living cannot be gainsaid. What kind of ends are to be pursued and what must be avoided, what beliefs could be true and acceptable and what ones are false and must be rejected, what should be our approach to assess events and actions are questions which have to be continually asked. An open mind, broad horizon, loving disposition coupled with a realization of the finitude which characterizes human existence are likely to lead our quest in the proper direction.

The gains of such a constant self examination when percolate on the bringing up of children would naturally illumine the way which would reveal the proper objects of likes or dislikes and love and hate. It is possible to cull the essential insights from different cultures which encapsulate the experience of ages, enrich our mind and lend orientation to our quest. *Dhammapad, Annalects* of Confucious, *Gita, Sermon on the Mount,* Tao and similar texts abound in the guiding insights.

Love has often been understood as an intimate relation between two individuals – particularly between a man and a woman. Such a love involves physical intimacy. It is often implied that persons who would have such a relationship will remain loyal to each other in the sense that no one of them would have any physical intimacy with any other person. Such a concept seems to be largely prevalent in the monogamous relationships found anywhere on the globe. However there are several departures. First, frequently male members take the principle not very seriously though they require their spouses to be strictly loyal to them. Secondly, the teens confusing curiosity, desire and love often get into relationships which they later repent. As the permissiveness seems to be growing and contraceptives are within the easy reach, it is gradually becoming clear that the monogamous love which had no deviations earlier is being reduced to an 'ideal relationship' if not regarded a matter of antiquated history.

Desire for having children, having intimate physical pleasure and companionship are three separate components involved in a monogamous relationship. It is said desire to have children may dominate the relationship or may not.

For companionship the other two are not indispensable, while the physical intimacy sometime may or may not culminate into such a relationship. The nature seems to have designed physical intimacy for the perpetuation of race. These facts are generally not seen the way they seem to be operative. In any case, a more puzzling question emerges, when love is considered as cementing a larger number of people irrespective of gender considerations. The command 'love thy neighbour' indicates this kind of love. In India it has often been the case that saints have cared not so much about their own family members as they have cared for the humanity. The question is can we love all? Sometime it is said that even an enemy deserves our love. How does this love compare with the intimate love between the two people?

It might be conjectured that the intimate love between two persons is exclusive while the love for mankind is inclusive. In one case the physical intimacy seems to be intrinsic to the relationship, while in the other case it is the general concern for the other which is fundamental. In the exclusive love, there is feeling of possession which is dominant and operative, while in the other the other is allowed to be as free as anyone else. Of course, physical intimacy has nothing to do with this wider concept of love. It is also obvious that the wider concept has no room for hate, while the narrower concept gets dangerously close to

Reason and Unreason

"The heart has its reasons which reason does not know." Blaise Pascal.

We have generally eulogized ourselves as different from all other living species on the planet and have proudly proclaimed that we are rational. Man is a rational being. Is this true? Is it a justified claim? What does raising such questions indicate? What is truth? What does it mean to ask whether something is true? What do we mean by justification? Why do we raise questions relating to justification? What does it mean to ask whether something is justified? These questions seem to point to several important things. First there is some close relationship between being rational, something being true, something being justified. Rationality, truth and justification are closely related. Secondly, only a being endowed with rationality would raise questions of this kind. Human beings do all kind of things. But they also seek reasons for doing things. If they have done something they want to feel that what they have done has been right, in other words, they can produce reasons to justify their doings or acts.

This is also a fact, that everything that human beings do may not be supported by a reason. There may be causes for what they do. Their actions may be explained in terms of causes. But it may not be possible to justify what they do or have done. Sometime these causes are adduced as reasons for the action and this takes the form of justification. However, it is not obvious, if causal explanation can be called a justification. If a causal explanation could be treated as a rational justification, no action or doing could ever be called irrational or unjustifiable. But this is also a fact that we often act irrationally or what we do cannot be supported by any good reason.

In fact, this does not need any great research or investigation to show that human beings have often acted in a way which cannot be supported by any good reason. Indifference to simple rules of life and nature, having disregard for simple norms of appropriate relationship, planning to hurt or destroy fellow human beings, choosing crooked or long winded paths to reach destination desirable or undesirable, ignoring the right ways of livings and so on result into actions which are often destructive to the individual agent as well as to others. The well known saying of Krisna, that he comes on the earth whenever people deviate from right path, order and start committing sins, in order to punish them so that good people may feel protected and are not dismayed, shows that wrong doing is quite widespread amongst human beings. Is it still right to think that we human beings are rational beings?

We noticed that rationality has to do with truth and justification. We should further note that rationality is also related to order and harmony in society. Thus actions which disrupt order or affect harmony adversely amongst the people cannot be called rational. But the question is what is to be understood by order in the society. Harmony, of course, is different from order. In a broad way it may be suggested that order refers to something external while harmony has to do with the internal relationships. Absence of explicit conflicts and combats may mark order, while positive helpful feeling for each other or attunement may be taken to be indicative of harmony. Order, however, is not merely confined to the absence of conflicts and combats but it also explicates the structure of a society.

It is well known that the notions of order and structure are really normative concepts meant to regulate relationships in the society. The way in which they have been conceived and consequently the ways in which they have been attempted to be applied to human populations, has been changing from one period to another. There were times when it was taken for granted that a certain section of society would consist of slaves, blacks or *sudras*. Sometime it was also assumed that some people are born to rule while the rest have to be ruled. As we all know these ideas came to be rejected, though the kind of treatment to slaves or sudras they led to still prevails in some way or the other.

While order and structure are normative notions they depend for their content on certain values which relate to the place of human beings in the society. The place of a human being in the society is determined by the concept of a human being which has been accepted in the society. Normally all human beings should belong to someone domain or class. They can only be contrasted with other living beings. In theory, at least in our times, all human beings are supposed to be treated as equal. Unfortunately, in practice and in actuality, all kinds of differences are introduced amongst them. As is said, some are treated as more equal and some are treated less equal.

Since order, structure and norms and the form of a society are two sides of the same coin, it has often been emphasized that it is the culture of a society which would determine what counts to be rational in that society. If the ideas, thinking and behaviour of an individual are in conformity with the prevailing norms of a culture, that individual would be called rational. What does not conform to one's culture and what one confronts in the ways of living of the people belonging to some other culture, is often a matter of ridicule and is considered to be irrational? It is only as a result of mutual understanding of cultural diversity that people come to realize that people of a different culture live differently and there is nothing ridiculous or irrational about life style. One would wish such a mutual understanding to be much more widespread than it is for it is its absence which leads to suspicion, insecurity, hatred and intolerance.

Within one/s culture different domains relating to different aspects of society lead to different ways of understanding rationality. Rationality as we noted, has to do with the type of objectives which give direction to behaviour. Not only the typology of the objectives, it is also important as to what ways and methods one adopts to achieve or attain them. Consider the economic aspect. The notion of production and profit dominates economic thinking. The notion of development is largely worked out keeping an eye on the interests of those who are involved in such a planning. Of course, public interest serves to veneer the whole project.

It is evident that the production and profit depend on the consumption habits of the members of the society. However, the commercial interests not only reinforce these habits but also generate new wants to proliferate production in immense variety. The economic well being is understood in terms of per capita income, quality of productions, and absence of unemployment. There may be many more things to be added to these points, but one can understand, that the economic rationality would be understood in terms of the economic well being and the ways to attain it. Basically it is calculative and instrumental rationality.

Similarly, in the domain of politics, well being of a society would depend on how well a certain polity is governed, to what extent people participate in the process of decision making, whether the rights of citizens are respected, whether the government is able to maintain law and order in the country and defend it against the possible or actual invasions, and so on. These objectives would depend on who are elected and how they are elected to run the show. For an efficient, people friendly government, it is essential that those who govern have the objectives of general welfare and development of material conditions of the society as the guiding principles. The consideration of the objectives and the ways by which these would be attained would determine the idea of political rationality. What really people experience actually, is some kind of opportunism which vitiates the entire function of polity. The players have an eye on their individual gains, and consider only that to be rational which is conducive to their narrow ends. Rationality as it ought to obtain and rationality as it is understood by the agent seem to be different from each other.

One can think of the way rationality is understood and practiced in other domains of society on these lines. The main thing to be understood is what counts to be rational or what are taken to be good reasons to support some idea, policy or action is determined by the type of the objective and the ways to attain it. If these objectives remain confined to the narrow ends of the individuals and if it is assumed that anything is right which would enable one to attain such an objective, we have one type of rationality. Thus if the individual were left to oneself one would think that it is perfectly rational to think of one's own well being and also to work for its attainment. Looked at from the point of view of the larger group, such as family, institution, or society as whole, such a rationality may conflict with the welfare of such a group and may not be considered as rational at all.

Thus it becomes extremely important to exercise proper discretion when choosing an objective. This requires an awareness of the fact that the welfare or well being of an individual is bound up with the welfare and the well being of the other individuals or society as a whole. Not merely choice of the objective, it is also important to be aware of the consonance of means with ends. To neglect this consonance would be to opt for mere instrumental rationality. This would vitiate the nature of the end itself. This was one great insight which Gandhi wanted people to realize.

Rationality is said to be related to the faculty called reason. Human beings are supposed to be endowed with various higher functions of mind, such as reason, intellect, intuition, memory imagination and will et cetera. They enable us to think, imagine, construct, and will. The way we use these terms sometime leads us to think that these are all independent faculties and are different from each other. There are several questions which arise at this point. Are these faculties totally independent of each other? That is, if one is active then the other is not. Where can they be located? How are they related to senses? Do they function without the aid of senses? Can they be ranked as lower and higher? Let us look for the answers in the two different traditions – Indian (more specifically Hindu) and Western.

We should notice that Indian thinking is radically different from the Western one, when mind is compared with body. In West, mind is conceived as separate and independent of body. Body is considered to be material. Mind is considered to be non-material. Mind, reason, intellect, understanding are often used synonymously. Intuition, memory, imagination and will are also comprehended within the notion of mind. Sometimes reason is used interchangeably with spirit or soul. So far as the Indian concept is concerned there seem to be two different approaches. Sometimes senses, reason, and spirit or *atma* are spoken as if indicating stages of the same continuity. In other words there is no qualitative distinction between senses and higher stages. But the more dominant view is that the mental faculties that is, senses, *manas* and intellect (*buddhi*) are distinct from soul or *atma*. They are called '*antah-karana*'. However, like senses they too fall within the domain of what is called *prakrti*-an unconscious principle. In the Sankhyan system of Indian thinking, *prakrti* is supposed to be material when compared with '*purusa*'. *Purusa* is purely non-material principle or entity. In Advaita Vedant also *antahkaran* is considered to be as material. In both the cases they are distinguished from gross matter as subtle matter.

Thus mental faculties as falling within the domain of *prakrti* are all material. Because of this belief there arises a problem in the Sankhyan system, how can knowledge be possible if these mental faculties are material, for knowledge is a conscious system, and consciousness is not material. Only purusa is conscious. Another problem would be the location of these faculties. If they are material they should be tangible and identifiable. They have been conceived as internal limbs, and perhaps they may have been accompanied with the idea that it could be possible to locate them somewhere inside the body. The medical texts – Caraka and Susruta, mention '*hrdaya*' that is heart. It is sometimes also called '*mana*'. And *mana* is rendered in English as mind. There is even a mention of *atma* being located in *hrdaya* and is said to be as big as a thumb. There is no mention, however, of the identification of this part in the body.

In Western thinking, there has been a problem relating to senses and reason in the context of knowledge. There have been several approaches in respect of the functions of these two in the context of knowledge. Some have considered the role of senses as dominant and fundamental so far as the possibility of knowledge is concerned. The role of reason has been considered ancillary in the sense that once the data is available to mind through the senses, reason proceeds to operate on it. It proceeds with abstraction, generalization, finding relations, analyzing the different components, comprehending them in a whole and so on. Some have considered the role of senses only as incidental. According to this view the function of senses merely indicates the occasion when the mind encounters the world and knowledge ensues. What is taken to be as an object in the external world is really a mental construct? Such a view is attributed to Idealist thinkers.

Still another view considers the role of senses as much important and fundamental as that of reason or mind. According to this view for the given, data or the object one has to depend on the senses. Without there being something given or some manifold the question of knowledge does not arise. But the given, manifold or the data comes to consciousness as a construct having been comprehended under some categories of the mind. Everyone knows that knowledge has a quantitative aspect. It increases. Whenever there is knowledge, something new comes to be added to the store. But knowledge is not considered knowledge if it is not reliable, if there were no necessity in it for being what it is. Such a thing could not have been possible if mind had not contributed to it. This has been the famous insight contributed by Immanuel Kant.

There has been another context in which the relationship between senses and reason has posed a serious problem. We may call this context as that of practical reason, or that of choice and action. It is to be noted that the cognitive aspect is not dissociated with this context. Senses are held to be responsible for the degradation of man; they are seen as the source of unreason. First, they often deceive us as to what is real; secondly they contribute to undesirable attachment to the things of this world which involves us in undesirable doings. While we learn about the world through the senses as to what is there and how it is, we also feel good or bad about the objects and events in the world. Sensations apprise about the world on the one hand and they also indicate our affective reaction to them. When we see things we find them ugly or beautiful, pleasant or unpleasant. When hear voices or sounds we find them cacophonous or sonorous. Our smell informs about the quality of things and determines whether we would proceed towards them or move away from them. Thus, through senses we come to be attracted to things or are repelled by them.

The attraction to things creates a desire to possess them, consume or enjoy them. These desires sometime get so intense that all other considerations become insignificant and the agent gets into a state of strong craving of getting hold of the object by any means. That is why such a desire is called a passion. For the agent is under the sway of the object to such an extent that s/he becomes completely passive. It is the things which determine what the agent would do. The agent herself or himself looses all reason or control and is charmed by the object. The consequences of the action are no more in the consciousness. The idea of fairness or unfairness becomes inoperative.

Since senses, (at least in the external aspect) are parts of the body, it is the body which has to take all the blame. It should be noted that notwithstanding the critique of senses, it is not the external aspects of them which are actually functional. It is their internal anatomical structure and physiology which explain how they function. In Indian thinking, it is said that it is inner power or energy which determines their function. It is clear that if the function of the senses is to be traced to the internal anatomy and physiology, it is basically the bodily features which are being considered as determining the functions of the senses. So far as intellect, reason or conscience is concerned though they are considered to belong to human personality yet they are not open to external observation. That is why they were called 'antah karan'—internal organs. It is a different matter that the question of their being located and identified within the inside of the body has remained problematic.

The brain-imaging is supposed to explain some aspects of the higher functions of mind. The structure of brain consists of two hemispheres of the brain, mid brain, thalamus, hypothalamus, hippocampus and amygdala. These are spots which are associated with thought, language, emotions, memory et cetera. But we yet do not know which part is to be called reason or which part is to be called conscience, or where consciousness is to be located. The quest is open. It would be immature and prejudicial to declare that these higher aspects of mind cannot be located in the brain for certain. This much is clear that to associate senses alone with body and to associate mental functions with spirit or soul (at least from the Western point of view) only, would perhaps be not correct. This consideration casts doubt on the compartmentalization between spirit and matter.

We have noted that in Indian thinking, at least in one stream, both types of functions that of senses as well as those of mind are said to belong to the domain of *prakrti* that is matter. There the distinction has been introduced as consciousness and what is devoid of consciousness. *Purusa* as we noted is supposed to be indicative of consciousness while prakrti has been taken to indicate all that which is devoid of consciousness. Although it has not been clearly explained as to how the functions of mind would be possible in the absence of consciousness, or alternatively, if they function as seemingly being conscious, how does that become possible, if the distinction between atma or spirit and matter has been accepted. We must, however, remember that the distinction between spirit and matter, while it can be said to be maintained both in West and East, does not actually mean the same thing in the two contexts.

Reason, as can been seen, seems to be endowed with a privileged position as compared to senses. But how is it to be understood in itself? Philosophers have talked of theoretical reason and practical reason. Theoretical reason is supposed to sort out the given, to abstract and generalize and fix concepts and principles, to differentiate and analyze the various components in the given, to fix the place of a component in the whole, and to enable us to visualize the whole itself. Practical reason is supposed to guide us about our actions – how should they be done, what should be their direction. What should be our duties and how should we behave. Apart from these two major areas, reason is also supposed to be concerned with the explanation of natural events, that is, how certain conditions lead to certain other conditions. Such an understanding is also essential for performance of any action. The agent should know beforehand as to what method or procedure would enable her or him to attain a certain end. In this third and the last function it would appear that reason is not so much concerned with the nature and worth of ends, as with the way to attain them. Such a function of reason is called instrumental.

We should not think that all these three functions operate as distinct from each other. It is quite possible that in a project all of these may operate in some way or the other. One is reminded of the dilemma which Arjuna is supposed to have faced while he was placed in the mid of two armies in Kuruksetra. As we learn from the *Gita,* Arjuna needed proper knowledge and some wisdom in order to get rid of his despondency. He also needed constant encouragement to get up and be ready for the fight. He had to realize why the war had become unavoidable, and that the just order was at stake, and finally that he could surrender all his worries to Krisna, for in fact it was the divine force which was at work and Arjuna was merely an efficient cause in the event. These features indicate how the various aspects of reason are operative together. Arjuna already had the skills needed for a successful combat. He was fully aware of the 'how to' aspect. He was disturbed by the consequences of a war. He was not going to fight for the first time. In fact he knew about the consequences of a war and yet he had fought many of them earlier and had won them. But this time his near and dear ones were involved in it and he would have to fight with them In order to be emancipated from this anxiety he needed right kind of understanding of the ultimate nature of the being and self. This can be taken to be the cognitive function of reason. Krishna told him that he must fight because it was his duty without considering any other thing. This was the function of practical reason.

Sill the three functions of reason can be clearly distinguished from each other. The theoretical and instrumental functions are allied. They are mainly concerned with the knowing aspects – knowing that or what, and knowing how. By theoretic function we learn how things are and how they behave. In this domain it is description and explanation which are main operations of reason. The practical reason is concerned mainly with why and ought. As a rational being a human being has to act with deliberation and justification. S/he should be aware of the causal relation in order to be able to perform an action. S/he must further be convinced of the worthiness of the ends of the action. S/he must have a sense of duty and should be able to perform the action just because it is her or his duty to do so. Thus it is the notion of justification which is crucial in the domain of practical reason.

That we raise questions about reason, we raise questions about action, we raise question about explanation and justification, that we raise questions of this sort distinguishes us from all the rest of the living beings. Perhaps, it can also be said that we raise questions of this sort because we have reason. This voice of reason blares in the interrogative 'why'. The most intriguing aspect is why we human beings slip away from this essential characteristic which defines us. Or we have failed to understand ourselves properly? Once again, let us go back to the war at Kuruksetra. Arjuna had almost surrendered his reason, for he confessed that he did not know what he should do and what he should not do. If there were no Krisna to take care of Arjuna, it was quite likely that he had abdicated his duty. Such a thing happens when one is faced with considerations which seem to point in two different directions. It does not seem to be clear as to which direction would be the right direction. It should be noted that an awareness of conflict in the alternatives is itself indicative of the presence of reason. If reason were not there, we would not be aware of any conflict.

But the analysis of the conflict as presented in *Gita* indicates that there are certain beliefs which derive their force from the attachment that we have to persons, things and events. Such attachment disables us to perceive the situation in which we are placed correctly. In our day to day life, incidents can be found without number which can illustrate how our attachment to things or persons, drives us towards actions, which in cooler and calm condition we might find we ought not to have done. Does it mean that attachment by itself is something wrong or evil and should be avoided altogether? If there is no attachment whatsoever can one at all act? Is it possible to act only because we think that we should act?

Before attempting an answer to these questions, let us think what is just and what is not just. Justice or fairness presupposes duality or plurality of human beings. If I am the only being and there is no other being besides me then no wider context is involved, there would be no meaning to the concepts of justice or fairness. It is because there are more beings than one that the question of justice and fairness arises, in other words, to be unfair to the other is not to be concerned with her or him, to be indifferent to her or his rights, pains and comforts. To be fair, on the contrary, would mean, proper and fair distribution of goods and services let us say. These considerations point to an important fact about justice and fairness. They presuppose ontology of pluralism – presence of more individuals than one. On the other hand the source of unreason may also be traced to pluralism. If one takes the other as so distinct from oneself that there is nothing absolutely common between the two, then also problems would arise. In *Kathopnisad* we are told that seeing difference is ignorance or false knowledge, not only this, one who sees differences is bound to move from one death to another or from one life to another (2.1.10). Justice and fairness presuppose the fact of equality of all human beings which in turn would presuppose some kind of oneness amongst them. Paradoxically speaking, seeing oneness in all beings can also prevent from injustice or evil being done, for if everyone is considered as oneself, there can be no other and therefore there can be no enemy or evil doer.

Perhaps the intent underlying the perception of unity amongst all living beings, is not to deny the ontological plurality of beings but to render empathy possible and thereby strengthen the feelings of the concern for the other beings in the same way as one would have for oneself. The truth of the saying found almost in all cultures that do to the others what you would to do to yourself comes into relief when the unity of all beings is realized.

Whether it is reason or unreason, for the function of either, a pluralistic world is a necessary presupposition. The notion of attachment, as we noted, has been described as the source of unreason. We have also noted that without desire the action would not be possible. This shows that attachment cannot be given up altogether. What needs to be seen and done is to see that one seeks pleasure or fulfillment not at the cost of the other. Narrow interest should not be allowed to be oblivious of the larger interest of humanity.

In scientific reasoning, empirical evidence, deductive reasoning and quantification in mathematical mode are supposed to be basic components in the methodology. We also learn from the history of scientific discoveries that insight and intuition have also played a significant role. It should be noted that insight or intuition has worked as a clue rather than as justification. In contrast to scientific reasoning, faith means relying on a statement – available as either heard or in written form, without questioning or seeking justification. No justification is sought for the authority of the speaker or the writer is accepted as unquestionable. This may be because the speaker or the writer is an expert on the subject, or is known for her or his reliable character.

There is another more significant argument supporting reliance on faith and that is the supposition that certain objects, events or religious beliefs are beyond the can of understanding. Not all that exists or is real can be accommodated in the empirical or phenomenal realm. But for believers of different denominations the realm beyond the phenomenal or empirical is not merely real but the only real. As compared to such a reality which is often mentioned with a capital 'R', the empirical or phenomenal reality is subsidiary or of second rate if not illusory.

Believers argue that human reason is finite and limited in its understanding and reach and so must not intrude on the realm of faith. Such a faith has played a very significant role in the lives of believers, giving them support in hard times and their miseries and has given them strength to face the odds in life. But it has also led to in-groupings, exclusiveness, alienation, hostility, and violence. One may retort that such a view is distorted and has nothing to do with real faith which generates love and concern for humanity. However, the negative and destructive facts associated with religion cannot be gainsaid.

It is quite remarkable that in this age of scientific and technological progress the adherence to religious beliefs and practices in different religions of the world has also increased. Even the great scientists sometime at the height of their career tend to be inclined to some sort of mysticism. The paradox is that while the religious people wish to show the limitation of reason, yet they argue for such a conclusion relying on reason. Similar experience of two believers may turn out to be a bond between them, yet for communication or dialogue between two persons the role of reason and rational approach cannot be minimized. It is only in terms of reason that wise people differentiate between superstition and wisdom.

Thought and Action

"What is the hardest task in the world? To think."
R.W.Emerson

No one would deny that we human beings are finite beings. We are born, we live for some time and then we die. This is the brief story of each of us. Life is short and art is long. We keep on knowing and learning throughout our lives though often we delude ourselves in believing that we know all that there is to be known and we have learnt everything that can be learnt. Most of the time, most of us allow no time delay in our reactions. We respond almost immediately to an utterance, a gesture, behaviour or whatever happens there in nature or to the objects that we confront. Sometime it is the need of the moment that an immediate reaction or decision is required. However, often we are in a situation in which we need to deliberate before acting or reacting. There is an ancient Indian saying, measure well your words before you speak. The same would apply to action. One should deliberate well before acting.

Actions may be simple or complicated. They may require minimum of effort or they may be long drawn out. One may be able to consummate an action by oneself from the beginning to the end. One may require help of others to bring an action to its finish. An action may have its origin in the biological or psychical need of the individual or in some feature related to some external circumstance or situation. An action may have to be carried out as a dictate of some powerful or authoritative personnel or it may be a consequence of the deliberation of the doer or several people belonging to a certain cohesive group.

There are activities going on constantly within the body which support life and bodily movements of which the individual is not conscious at all. Only an expert with the help of certain instruments can find out what is going on inside the body. There are bodily movements which occur automatically as a response to some stimulus of which the individual is either not aware or is only vaguely aware. All these activities may be directed activities having some purpose or function relating to the maintenance of the body but of which we are not aware nor need be aware. These activities do not require any cerebral exercise – thinking or deliberation in order to arrive at a decision. We are not conscious of them. They are thoughtless.

There are well deliberated actions which sometime invite the invective of 'thoughtless action'. Actions which are guided by narrow and immediate interests which ignore the wider contexts and concern for others and remote consequences lead to results showing their thoughtlessness. Such an invective would be justified if the consequences of selfish action turn out to be destructive for some or all concerned. However, in daily routine, most of our actions have got to be limited to our immediate concerns or necessities. In the course of practice or frequent repetition one may not require deliberation before acting, but in most cases concentration and continuous watch over what we are doing, whether as a trifle or something very serious is necessary for the proper performance of the action.

It may escape our notice that action is an external manifestation of thought. An action does not merely involve thought, but it also depends on numerous internal bodily functions which of course do not occur in our consciousness. One needs some strength and stamina in terms of the activity of the various parts of the body – such as the activity of muscles, joints, nerves and so on, to enable an individual to act. It is only in the case of some physical disability or malfunction that we realize that the internal physical activity has some role in our bodily movement and thereby in our action. In what direction and in what form the external activity would take place will depend on the cerebral activity and also on the state of the inner function of the body. The internal and external appear to indicate only the two phases of the same process. Thus thought and action can actually be seen as continuous. Thought may be considered as preceding an action and an action as following the thought.

Does this continuity imply that there is a consonance between thought and action? Do not we often find that the actions are not in consonance with the thoughts or beliefs that an individual holds? What goes on in the green room behind the stage where the form and direction of the action is determined? The green room does not seem to be as tidy and orderly as we find the stage. It seems to have several people each of whom seems to force himself for attention. Even at the conscious level the individual agent may feel some sort of conflict between the ideas or beliefs s/he has before s/he decides to act. S/he may feel the force of each of these conflicting ideas. The nature of the conflict depends on various constellations of which these ideas form part. Some may be connected with what the individual desires. Some may be associated with what the individual thinks as to what he ought to desire. Some actions may have their origin in some external pressure directed from the position of some sort of power. Some may be related to the availability or non-availability of resources or means to carry through the action. Some others may be spurred by the desire to express or to actualize some fancy, experience or vision.

While these various pressures may attend the deliberations of a person while he is in a process to take a decision, only that part of these ideas would be continuous with the action which actually forms part of the resolution and which shapes and directs the action. Keeping this consideration in mind, it seems to be plausible to say that there is a continuity to be found between thought and action. The idea of continuity between thought and action prevents us from treating the two as diametrically opposed to each other. In a sense, such a view also prevents the widely held distinction between mind and body. Body is the stage where the action is played out. The drama played out as action is exposed to an audience. One can see it, film it, record it and show it. It is obvious that some part which constitutes the drama remains hidden from the audience.

However, the audience can guess what is going on in the minds of the actors on the stage by what they do and say.

Moving further in the history of action, it would be found that only some segment of the consequences of the action is continuous with the thought(in terms of intention of the agent), if at all. Every action has intended and unintended spill outs. The actual consequence may not match with the intended consequences. It is possible that partly or wholly the actual consequences may not be what the agent intended. This, of course, is not necessary that it may turn out that what the agent intends does not fructify. What is to be noted is that the consequences of the action may have several possibilities some of which may or may not match with the intention of the agent. In the unintended consequences the chain of reactions should also be included. In fact, an action has a beginning in some motive or intention, but if one becomes inquisitive about the origin of the motive or intention itself, the history of the action will have to be pushed further backward. Similarly, though seemingly an action appears to come to an end in some changes in the state of affairs, it may keep on causing further chain effects which nobody bothers to record normally, which may even escape the notice of the agent.

At least two important features come to mind in respect of unrecorded or un- noticed consequences of an action. First, that in most cases an action has a tendency to repeat itself. It is a different matter that other motives or inclinations prevail and the tendency to repeat may go in the background for the time being. Secondly, normally we take into account the action of only some one agent. It is likely that similar actions are performed by several agents either at the same time or on different occasions. This sort of thing may result into a cumulative effect which may come to notice like the emergence of a big wave in the ocean. Such a thing happens when a mob acts. Again the action may be a part of bigger plan to be carried through by a number of agents. We might think of corporate action in the realm of production, in an institutional framework, in a combative strategy and the like. These considerations point to the fact that the micro unit of the continuity of thought and action is a local happening in a vast drama of events.

From a different point of view it seems that thought and action will have to be viewed as discontinuous. It can be said that thought must stop if action is to begin. This position appears to contradict whatever we have speculated about thought and action so far. This requires us to pause and watch for what is happening when we think that we think. The first thing to notice is that thinking indicates a process which is different from a reverie or a mere free flow of ideas or images. One looks for some sort of connectivity between two ideas or thoughts. The flow of ideas in thinking seems to be controlled. Just as I would choose a certain path in order to arrive at a certain destination, I try to move through the connected ideas to a certain conclusion. There is one important difference in my moving towards a known destination and moving towards a certain idea of which I may or may not have any idea.

I may be looking for a solution to a problem, or an answer to some question, or how certain ideas relate with each other, or what follows from certain given ideas, what kind of organization be introduced in a bunch of ideas, could they be arranged in a sort of hierarchy, or some sort of mutual relationship and so on. It is obvious that this activity cannot go on if there are no ideas to be entertained. But then where do I get these ideas from? Rene Descartes, a French Philosopher, told us that we possess some of them just because we have a mind, some of them we acquire by our encounter with our surroundings, and the rest may be a result of free play or regulated activity of mind in which our imaginative skill has a major role. There is another way to think about the origin of ideas. We have a huge number of them like impressions of what we encounter. They may be compared with pictures that we shot through a camera. But there are ideas which do not resemble anything that we encounter. It seems that our mind is so designed that it generates ideas to deal with the ideas that we acquire as a result of our encounter with the world. These ideas are different from the ideas which they organize.

If I find one thing as different from the other, I have an idea of 'difference'. This idea would not arise if there were no two things dissimilar to each other. If I find a face resembling the other I have an idea of 'resemblance'. There are many ideas like that of difference and resemblance and with them mind is able to work with the ideas that it acquires. Ideas like 'difference', 'resemblance', and 'identity' and so on as applied to certain other sets of ideas can be distinguished from them as forming a different class. The most interesting and amazing activity of mind is in its creativity in the sense that it forms and generates entirely new ideas with its imaginative ingenuity and thereby changes, modifies, and adds to the world. The simplest form of such an activity can be noticed in our numerous day to day activities involved in the process of our living and survival. Our imaginative activity is propelled by the needs that we feel which have to do with living and living well. (The unpacking of the notion of 'well' would lead us into several directions and cannot be taken up right now.)

Our needs and interests move us to look for things which agree with us and leave the others. When we do not find a thing which we need or in which we are interested then with the help of our imaginative capacity and experience we make or create things out of the existing material which did not exist in the form we gave to them. In this process we also choose the way, method or the technique to proceed with our design. There are not merely things but certain state of affairs which we would like to be there and which either are not there or not in good shape, for example, the state of garbage in the locality in which we live, which we would wish not to be there. To bring such state of affairs about requires a long and complicated strategy. There are however, very simple situations, such as closing or opening the window, where such complicated strategies are not needed.

Such activities involving complicated strategies require lot of deliberation. We think of several alternatives involving problems relating to labour, time, space, consent of other people and their cooperation, the feasibility and desirability of the project, from the point of view of an individual and also from the point of the community. For the moment we are keeping aside the considerations which may be of selfish and narrow interest and which may intervene and distract us from the right and proper strategy. In these cases ideas of rejection and acceptance have a crucial role. These ideas go with ideas of choice and freedom on the one hand and desire and interest on the other. They are different from the ideas of difference and resemblance in this that they sort of move us into some activity or the other.

Let us for the time being concentrate on these two types of ideas – those relating to observation and those relating to doing. We may observe matters as long as possible and as many of them as possible or from as many angles as possible. Similarly we can think and consider of as many alternative as we can find and we can think and consider about their costs and pay offs in as many ways as possible. So far as, our thinking and consideration and deliberation are concerned, we may go on in our search without limit. We seem to be completely free in such an activity for it all goes on in our mind. This can be carried on even when I am confined to a cage.

But this activity will have to be cut short, suspended if not completed, when the situation demands me to make a move. I have to decide and resolve and finally act. The necessity to act puts a pause if not a full stop to my thinking activity. But let us be careful. Stopping the thinking activity does not mean that the cognitive processes would cease to operate. Action requires that I keep my eyes open, my senses receptive. I have to keep an eye on every step that I am required to take in the process of action. This shows that the thinking has not completely stopped and this also shows some kind of continuity of thought and action for I am to be continuously aware of the destination, the steps in between and whatever else is necessary to move in that direction. Yet there is a sense in which the activity of thought has come about. Such an activity of thinking is concerned with exploring the alternatives and their costs and benefits at thought level.

Readers might be reminded of the idea of acting and being indifferent about the results as propounded in *Gita*. When Arjuna would be on the battle ground and would be engaged in the active fight he cannot afford to act blindly or without thought. He has to be careful about the target he is supposed to hit, he has to calculate the force with which the arrow is to be shot, he should be further aware of the mantra which he may have to invoke before shooting the arrow, and be ready for the next step. All this cannot be done without thinking, without observing the situation on the field which may be continuously changing and yet he has to suspend all thought of what could have come out of it, or what other alternative he could have chosen, or what could have been the other possibilities. Thought and action treated as inside and outside are phases of the same activity – part of it is visible to the other and part of it is not visible to the other. For the agent however the perspective is different. The agent, of course, is aware all through what is going on in her or his mind and in what direction and in what way s/

he is moving. Thus thought and action are both continuous and discontinuous.

Action and its results serve as a comment on thinking. In an obvious sense, if the expectations and outcome match, expectations will be considered as right and proper. On the contrary if the outcome does not match expectations then either something must have been wrong with expectation or the action. The whole process would require a close examination if the failures are not to be repeated. Perhaps, not all the relevant components relating to the objective and the means to attain them were not considered, something escaped attention or was not considered necessary. Or some calculations did not fit. May be the agent has been over confident and that may have led to carelessness. On the other hand while the action was undertaken some steps were missed, or some wrong turn led to miscarriage and so on.

Students of science know the importance of experiments in order to test a hypothesis. Experiments either support the hypothesis or lead to its rejection or modification, but the experiment must have been well designed and properly carried through. Scientific theories are either strengthened by practice or experiment or weakened. There is, obviously, very intimate relationship between theory and practice.

In the realm of morals, as in actuality, often a disparity is found between the precept and the percept. Thinking, utterances, and actions often reveal inconsistency and dissonance. In politics (not in the sense of citizenship), a degenerate realm of morals, it is hard to find a proper match between what the leaders say and promise and what they do and practice. In fact, some agents assimilate the disparity between what they say and do, into a planned clever policy. Those who find it difficult to suppress the voice of their conscience may be hard put to justify a wrong or unjust action. Let us make a note of a difference between two types of disparities between thought and action. Earlier we were concerned with the mismatch within what we planned and what actually was the outcome. In the other case, that is, in the moral realm, the disparity is found in the promises and performance. In most cases such a disparity is supposed to characterize a successful strategy of living in the world. It is taken for granted that promises are not meant to be kept. Deception becomes an accepted part of successful living.

Those who do not bother about the remote consequences of what they do and are lost in the indulgence of immediate gains, fail to see that they may be victim of similar attitude and behaviour of other people. It is easier to locate a contradiction in what one says or thinks, but very difficult to be aware of the contradiction if everyone has deception as part of his strategy. The amazing thing is that the person who deceives counts on the fairplay on the part of the other person involved. It does not occur to her or him that the other one may have a similar approach to things.

Man has often been defined as a rational being. To a great extent this saying has been vindicated by the progress human beings have made in understanding the laws of nature on the one hand and in the establishment of institutions and traditions to bring about order, cohesion, harmony and orientation amongst themselves on the other hand. Yet there are two important exceptions which jeopardise the validity of these statements. While human beings are endowed with a capacity to identify and locate contradictions and inconsistency, the beliefs that are stored in the mind do not make a coherent and consistent whole. A large chunk of mind seems to be a junk house where all kind of things are lying in a haphazard manner. Looked at from the point of view of psycho-analysis a store of the repressed or suppressed desires it is also called as id. Thus it has belief- like items and also impulse - like items. Perhaps this is also the source of imaginative force. Such a chunk of mind cannot be identified as a rational system.

Secondly if we consider human beings in collectivity, it would be found to be composed by people of all kind of dispositions, attitudes, capacities and deportments. Some would be rule minded while others may be rule breakers. Some may have bossing tendency while others might be meek and submissive. Some may be very capable and talented while some others may be slow and dull. Some may be found to be hatching conspiracies as to how to destroy and disturb the system, while some others may be found to be planning for a better organization. Some may have the attitude to serve while some may be interested only in being served. This description seems to imply that the individuals have fixed and typical profiles. That would be wrong. Like all things people are subject to change. However, that introduces some more complexity in the structure of the grouping. Such a mix allows us to see why we have so many problems pestering humanity. In a generalized way we might say that we ourselves are the source and origin of all our miseries. This is another exception to the belief that man is rational.

From what has been said, it is clear that rationality is being considered both in respect of cognitive structures as well as in relation to the dispositional and behavioural aspect. In both the cases it seems to be a regulative force which is not operative all the time. Many things that we think or do at the conscious level seem to ignore or defy reason. What we may do in private may be reprehensible in public. What we prohibit in the in-group is permitted in relation to the out-group. Notice that we have all kinds of in-groups each can be determined by the possessive 'my' – myself, my family, my friends, my school, my locality, my city, my state, my country and so on.

Thinking is very often understood in terms of epistemic and logical processes. Thinking about things in terms of 'this' and 'here', that is their particularity, or attending to their similarities and thereby to the common factor/s and thus arriving at a general or universal concept, or grouping things in terms of their common characteristic under a class concept are some of the main features of epistemic processes. They permit the activity of analysis and synthesis and thereby help in bringing about some kind of organization in whatever we come to know. Moving from one proposition to the other on the basis of some kind of connection, or trying to find out the implication/s of some proposition, in the sense that if we accept it what else will have to be accepted, or follows from it, are some important aspects of logical thinking.

Acceptance implies rejection, at least setting aside or being indifferent. To accept something involves a choice though it may be based on some factors which are already accepted or considered worthy of acceptance. As is obvious, choice would mean leaving out alternative positions or items. Attending some objects would mean that certain other objects are not being attended to. But the most interesting aspect of thinking is the difficulty in accepting two such items which are opposed to each other in some sense. In abstract way it is easy to understand that p and not p cannot go together or cannot be accepted. but when confronted with objects with multiple features where some aspects of the two things are in agreement or similar to each other, and other aspects do not agree with each other or seem to be utterly different, it is difficult to decide whether the two objects can be accepted together or not. This also indicates the difficulty in understanding the notion of contradiction which in a sense is basic to logic.

In the realm of action, when faced with two alternatives which possess some features which seem to be acceptable while some other seem to be unacceptable, one finds oneself in a conflicting situation and it becomes difficult to decide as to which alternative is to be followed. But there are other facets of thinking and doing which resist reduction into mere epistemic or logical processes. One thing which comes to mind is the fact that in actuality the processes of epistemic and logical thinking as dealt with in the academic context do not seem to be obvious in the verbal transactions though they may underlie these transactions. In actuality what goes on in the form of verbal transactions is accompanied with the emotional undercurrents, unreflective or spontaneous expressions and reactions, sometime backed by calculative motivations, but in the organized situations one can hope for precise, exact and to the point expressions.

But there are other contexts in which thinking or reflection takes place which are not strictly logical or epistemic though they may not be incompatible with them. In literature and arts, in politics and religious discourse, in market and gossip thinking acquires multicoloured dimensions. Within these contexts, two distinct orientations must be distinguished from each other. In one orientation, the thinking activity may not be to some definite purpose, for example, in the realm of poetry, music, and painting and allied arts. Purpose is extraneous to the aesthetic action and experience. But it may not be completely absent, for the artists are moved by the desire for appreciation, fame, and even money. Obviously these have nothing to do with writing a poem, singing a song or painting a picture. However, art may also be used for non-aesthetic purposes. It may be used for propaganda, publicity, inciting people to action in a certain direction. In such cases, the role of calculative thinking is obvious. Art may also serve as a political strategy. In fact, from the utilitarian point of view involving a concern for life and society, 'art for the art sake' is not always or highly appreciated.

These motivations are close to political, religious and marketing realms. In political and religious contexts, there is a tendency to attract people to certain interests, ideas, programmes and projects. Political parties count on the number of followers, the same is true of religious affiliations. In marketing this applies to the number of customers. Publicity and propaganda often appeal to reasons, scientific approach, utility, economic interests, even sensual pleasures. These are not utilized in the various contexts in the same way and in the same form. Perhaps it would be convenient to characterize thinking in these contexts as purely calculative and instrumental and obviously action oriented.

Lies, deceptions, distorted reasoning, and exaggerations, all these find their way into the propaganda tactics. They characterize calculative and instrumental thinking. But there are creative forms of thinking in which both imagination and insights have an intimate role. Such thinking helps in delineating the possible worlds manifesting better order and harmony. However, the aesthetic realm is not merely confined to visualizing possibilities. It allows for a critique of the present or the world as it is found. There is close link between such a critique and the notion of possible realms. While, the aesthetic realm is distinguished by the paradoxes of disinterested interest, purposeless purpose and an intrinsic state of being in which the object absorbs the subject, as a comment on life and world it also involves a reformative zeal. Aesthetic thinking moves through metaphors, analogies, and richness of meaning inherent in language rather than syllogisms. While epistemic and logical thinking are directed by generalization and abstraction, aesthetic thinking proceeds towards concretization and reification.

Often we hear of decisions made by corporate bodies. As already noted decisions imply deliberation and thinking. Thus the question arises, do corporate bodies think? Thinking is basically a characteristic of an individual. How can corporate bodies think? But it is also clear that people sit together and deliberate on issues. They talk the matter out. Ultimately they do arrive at some sort of consensus and that transforms into their decision. We may call such an activity as collective thinking. There is something quite significant to be discovered here. In actual collective thinking it may be found that individual interests and emotions intervene. However, if we visualize collective thinking in an ideal form, we would notice that the individuals contribute different perspectives or points of view and succeed in keeping their individual interests and prejudices in the background. It may be noticed that the progress in the cognitive enterprises has proceeded in the light of the ideal state of collective thinking and communication. Collective thinking helps in overcoming the limitations of the finitude of the individuals involved. Of course, a sincere desire to come to truth and a regard for the opinion of the other and permissibility of mutual criticism are unavoidable conditions for a collective discussion.

It is clear that there are any number of unavoidable activities which can be carried on only by the cooperative efforts of several people. Activities which an individual can perform with success are either very simple, rudimentary or partial in view of the collective activity. Thus we have collective thinking and also collective action. In this brief discussion we have found that there is very intimate relation between thinking and action – individual or collective, in the various contexts such as epistemic, logical, political, religious and aesthetic. It is possible to carry on deliberation indefinitely but it has to be suspended and decision has to be taken when the necessity of action is imminent. However, the direction and the manner of action would be determined by the deliberation. And in that respect it can be said that action is a phase in the same continuity of which thinking is an initial moment. That is why, perhaps, that action has been considered under the domain of practical reason.

Free or not free

'Our current picture of freedom encourages a dream like facility whereas what we require is a renewed sense of the difficulty and complexity of the moral life and the opacity of persons." Iris Murdoch.

'I was helpless. I had to do it. There was no other alternative.' Does this helplessness indicate that I was not free? It is said that one who is free can choose. In order to choose there must be alternatives to choose from. If there are no alternatives and there is no possibility of choice does that mean that there is no freedom? Perhaps not or rather one should think that there is no occasion to exercise freedom and therefore not free. When I had to act, I had to think of pros and cons. It appeared to me that the decision to act in a particular way was perhaps the best thing that I could do under the circumstances. But how did I weigh the pros and cons? Were not more than one possibilities open to me? Did I weigh every alternative carefully? Was I sure that these were the only alternatives available to me?

When thinking of the consequences, several kinds of considerations may occur, it may be loss or gain, name or shame, saving a close one or be unconcerned with one's safety, effects on others, duty or interest and so on. In short, it may be either a personal interest, or interest of the other or the desire or a sense of duty which helps me determine what course of action to adopt. The decision to do something or not do it is always open to me. But I may not deliberate at all before plunging myself into some act. I may be impulsive or just carried away. I may not know what I am doing. The idea of consequence may not occur to me at all. The desire or impulse may just make me blind.

Often this counts as an excuse for not acting deliberately. I was not within my control. But how such a thing comes about? Is it temperamental, habitual, or just because I did not train my self or was not trained to think before acting? Did I develop habits which prevented me to think before acting? Did I not learn to control my emotions and feelings and allowed my self to be swayed by them? These are questions which would be answered by different doers in different ways. But they do concern facts of life. This does happen that humans often act on impulse though they are endowed with a capacity to deliberate and decide. But does acting on impulse mean that I was not free to decide? One answer would be that the question does not arise. Acting with deliberation and acting on impulse are quite different things. Moreover, when it is said that the doer was swayed away, the doer was not under her or his control. In that case s/he was not free.

But one may ask why the doer was not under her or his control? As we have already noticed this question leads us to the personality make up of the individual and that in turn is determined by her or his dispositions which one has developed over a long period of time. It could also be urged that the personality make up is determined to a great extent by genes. But it has to be remembered that genes do not function in an exclusive way that is, without being modified by the effects of environment. Nature and nurture both determine the personality make up and both are responsible for the individual differences. So even if one argues that one was not in one's control, it could be held that one is responsible for the temperament one has developed.

But it may be that one finds no possibility to get out from a messy situation. One may be confronted by two exclusive alternatives and both may appear to be undesirable or potentially adverse in their consequences. Normally, in such a case one is advised, or one thinks to choose the less bad alternative. But it may happen that one may just not act. Does that mean that one was not free to act? It could be said that even not acting or not choosing is an act of deliberation and therefore, indicates the freedom of choice.

Another phenomenon which is very common to witness, is the fact that we do not wish to own an abrogated action or failure. We do sometime repent and try to understand why we failed in our effort. But mostly we tend to think that we couldn't help and it was because of the adverse circumstances that we failed or it was because of the other people that we were unsuccessful or it was our ill luck. On the contrary, if the action results into success we tend to attribute it to our own initiative and effort completely. The feeling 'I did it' boosts our confidence and ego. In some cases, particularly in a collective venture, we tend to appropriate the entire credit for success to ourselves. When we fail we think that we were not free and when we succeed we feel that we were free.

The success of collective ventures, as we notice, in technological action, depends not only on the mutual cooperation, but also on a very well thought out plan and strategy and consequent proper preparations. Such planning is backed by expert knowledge which has a long history. Unfortunately such a thing does not happen frequently in individual actions. We do not give enough thought to the matter at hand, or do not have enough relevant information, or the understanding of know how. Besides we also do not have full control on ourselves and are often tempted by an attractive object or immediate gain or get hurt even by legitimate criticism or lose our cool. As a consequence we act in haste or on impulse and our action turns out to be counter-active. These features obscure the issue regarding acting freely. It should be noted that a person is not excused if her or his action leads to consequences which are injurious to others. The law would treat such an action as a crime no matter in what situation it was committed. This indicates that in the context of social structure whatever a person does has to be attributed to her or his free will.

However, this is also a fact that often a criminal act remains unpunished if the crime is committed by a person holding a powerful (in whatever way, either because of money or status or muscles or sheer cleverness) position in the structure, while an ordinary citizen is easily caught. Apart from this, there are situations in which a person tries to follow the conventional rules of desirable behaviour and tries to rely on her or his hard work and honesty and yet suffers in all kinds of ways. Such a suffering is called undeserved suffering. Those who are not aware that such a suffering could be accounted for by the anomalous social situation or who do not reflect on such a cause, tend to attribute their suffering to fate.

But people have been long conscious of the conflict between *'purushkara'* (human effort) and *'daiva'* (divine dispensation). As mentioned above, people generally tend to attribute success to their own efforts and initiative while they explain away their failure by invoking the notion of fate or destiny.

It is also said that man proposes and God disposes. The deeper and sophisticated version of this saying is found in the principle that one should concentrate on one's duty and not on the consequences. It has been recognized that one has no control over the consequences, as we are taught by *Gita*. This is clearly a right understanding of the possible consequences on an action. There are two important points which crave our attention. First, our finitude – because of our finitude neither our information is ever fully complete, nor our capacities and abilities are full proof. As a result, though we are free to deliberate, decide and choose we are not fully in control of the perfection of our action. Secondly, we are not alone in the universe. There are other beings including human beings who are all engaged in action or activity of some kind or the other like us. Then there are forces independent of human volition, that is, natural forces. There is a sense in which our planet is a living planet. All kinds of movements are going on in nature on which we have very little control. Our action is not an isolated event. It tends to affect the world and the world has an effect on it. Thus, while, in practice, and in our day to day routine often we succeed in predicting the outcome, yet there are as many occasions when our expectations remain unfulfilled.

We act under numerous constraints and conditions. Some of these happen to be in our knowledge while there are many of which we are not aware. There are conditions which facilitate our action, while there are other conditions which act as constraints on our action. This is obvious that to perform an action it is necessary that our body is in proper health and our mental functions are active in a normal way. The conditions are favourable. Besides we are supposed to be aware of what we want, what are our objectives, and the possible ways by which we can attain those objectives? But there are other conditions of which we are hardly ever aware. When we walk or sit or hold something we do not know that it is gravity which makes these activities possible. If there were no oxygen available we would be choked and breathing would become difficult if not impossible. But when we breathe we do not realize that there is oxygen in the air. There may still be conditions of which we have no idea.

Similarly most of us do not know how the economic structure affects the quality of social structure. They have yet to devise a fully successful economic strategy which would give us a desirable (a debatable issue) social structure. Most of us, again, are not fully conversant with our traditions and heritage though we talk of them most of the time. Even if we know some part of our traditions and heritage we do not know which part should we follow in our life. The result is that we choose what suits us and our strategy. If we had properly and critically assimilated our traditions and heritage there would have been little scope for religious or communal disputes.

Freud believed that our mental structure consists of three parts – superego, ego and id. Id is that part of our mental structure of which we have absolutely no knowledge. We are not conscious of it. But it is a motivating force and keeps on affecting our desires and actions.

According to ancient Hindu beliefs, the results of actions in our past life continue to affect our desires and action, though these beliefs also included the belief that we are free to act in this life and we should not add to our past misdeeds. Buddha taught us that whatever happens happens according to a law (*pratityasamutpada*), that is, whatever happens is consequent on prior conditions and leads to further happening in a chain of events. Scientists tell us that there is a regularity in natural events and these events are ordered by causal relations. It is also said that it is the social conditions in which we have to live that we do what we do. Most crimes are explained by certain social conditions in which an individual finds herself or himself.

In *Gita*, Arjuna is told that, in actuality, he is not a doer or agent of his actions but a mere instrument in a divine plan. There is only one doer or agent and that is God Himself. There is another explanation which is different from this belief. In the same text we are told that whatever happens, because of human beings or otherwise, happens within the realm of three *gunas* – *satva, rajas,* and *tamas.* The realm of *gunas* is radically different from the realm of spirit/s. It is in this realm that all worldly happenings take place according to certain laws. In modern parlance one may think of nature in place of the realm of three *gunas.* The idea is also similar to the concept of phenomena as conceived by the German philosopher Immanuel Kant. What happens in the phenomenal realm happens according to rules which scientists discover. It is not possible to talk of free action in such a realm.

The question may arise if all these determining forces determine our behaviour, then where is the scope for us to determine our actions according to our will. Yet Krishna commanded Arjun to act and Kant made a room for free will. We should remember that the beliefs discussed in *Gita* and ideas discussed by Kant are, otherwise, very different in character from each other. For *Gita* though actions form a component in the realm of the three *gunas,* yet humans have to perform them for so long as they have bodily existence they cannot live without performing actions but they are advised to suppose that they are not the actual doers. For Kant every individual has a feature in her or his make-up which is independent of the phenomenal realm and it is because of this noumenal feature (noumenal world is not accessible to usual ways of knowing. It can only be thought of, as Kant believed.) Individuals exercise their will. However, like in *Gita,* Kant also considers a moral action moral when it is done with a sense of duty alone.

It is interesting to note that Kant has been taken to emphasize the notion of duty at the cost of feeling. One might think that it is possible to do good deeds out of good feelings. In *Gita* also it has been suggested that the individuals should rise about the feelings of pain and pleasure and even honour and condemnation. The question arises what would be human if human beings were devoid of feelings. Perhaps what is meant in both the contexts of Kant and *Gita,* is not that human beings are completely devoid of feelings, but only that feelings cannot be sure indication of right action alone.

What follows from this brief discussion is the idea that human beings though free in deliberating, deciding and choosing and consequently acting on their decision, they can do so only under some conditions as well as some constraints. In other words, there can be no unconditional freedom. By taking resort to helplessness, I can be absolved from the responsibility of what I do. But I must suffer the consequences. I must pay the cost of freedom which is inalienable.

It needs to be discussed as to how the notion of freedom works out in the social conditions. Apparently social constraints appear to contradict freedom of the individual. The issue requires a thought about the origin of social constraints – why are they needed, what is their justification. But first what is meant by the social constraints. These constraints have their source in the conventions embedded in the tradition of a certain society, in the legal system which has come to be evolved in order to maintain law and order in the society, in the rules which determine the membership of that society, and there may be others also. To whatever source these rules and constraints may belong they are basically meant to maintain peace and order amongst the members, so that they are able to live together in amity. But we all know that this aim remains a distant ideal and there is always a need of change or modification in the set of existing rules.

The root problem of most social issues may be reduced to the question, how to create or have an organization within which the interests of different individuals could be protected and realized without creating tensions and conflicts. The term 'interest' is very vague and may have various applications depending on the objectives of the individual implicit in the notion. Often what the individual takes to be in her or his interest is really not in her or his interest. A simple example is 'being tempted by immediate gains'. An action done under such a temptation later turns out to result in adverse consequences for the individual. But what about the well deliberated and well planned action which again is determined by the interest of the individual? Often it is found that individuals act on such a plan without taking into consideration the consequences of their action on others and the society as a whole. Such a neglect would not matter but for the fact that one has to live in the same society in which one carries out such a selfish plan, and one cannot avoid to be affected by the kind of society to which her or his action contributes.

Unfortunately most of us remain unaware of the remote consequences of what we do, and the effects our action has on others as well as on the surroundings in which we live. When more individuals follow such a strategy of action they are likely to act at cross purposes and sooner or later tensions and conflicts are bound to arise. The line of thinking which remains confined to ones own gains and profits often takes others as merely means to the fulfillment of one's objectives. Such a situation generates two major classes in the society – haves and have nots. Marxists and socialists have elaborated the issue and have discussed it threadbare. One important point that emerges from their vast researches and strategies is the idea that those who are exploited are free to resist exploitation and fight back against the exploiters. While apparently it appears that the oppressed is bound by his circumstances and is not free to live a life of human dignity, s/he is basically free to break away one's shackles. One is simply not aware of one's freedom because of which one does not find strength enough to resist and fight. So it was found necessary to make the exploited conscious about their freedom as well as the conditions under which they are exploited. Being aware collectively the exploited would attain solidarity and strength. Unfortunately such a struggle often results in the form of terror and violence. Yet it has brought about a change for good though it was not free from contradictions and problems. This has also shown that human beings are basically free to decide and act though they may have to suffer for their freedom.

On the other hand the last century has also witnessed an entirely different strategy for change though not primarily from the economic bondage. It was to break through the alien regime and was, theoretically, based on the principle of non-violence by an unusual man that is, Mahatma Gandhi. There were co-lateral movements for the same objective but were either indifferent to non-violence or thought it to be unfruitful. As we are all aware these movements resulted in the independence of India on August 15, 1947. The suit was followed by many countries in the world. All these movements were launched against powerful establishments in most cases political. Numerous people sacrificed their all including themselves. All these movements evince the fact that freedom cannot be curbed. Yet there are bondages other than those of political kind. The one which still persists is the economic bondage. Even today a huge segment of world population lives under poverty line. People still die of starvation. There are people who do not have even a roof on their head. They live and sleep on road side. Children beg and are even led into begging by unscrupulous criminals. A large percentage of children suffer from malnutrition. Tribals are being dislodged from their forest habitats. The construction of dams leads to displacement of population on a large scale and in spite of the claims of Government; many of the displaced persons do not get proper rehabilitation. There is unemployment on a large scale. Many degree holders fail to get suitable jobs. This situation has generated insurgency. In our country we read in the news papers about naxalites and maoists and so on. Their struggle involves lot of violence. So far poor governance has failed to gauge the situation and take adequate measures against it. However, for us the main thing to be noted is that if the insurgents did not feel free to act according to their strategy and were not aware of stakes they would not have dared to launch their struggle.

Isn't violence avoidable? Do not moves to change social conditions become counter-effective? Is it too much to expect to be governed well? The idea of democracy was a dream which generated hopes for equality in opportunities for all, everyone being treated as a person with rights and dignity and, of course, freedom for expression and work. Unfortunately for a large segment of people in the society still lives only by hope. The term 'politics' is no more a respectable term. It has little connection with civic sense or responsibility. On the contrary, politics has come to mean an opportunity to fulfill one's ends by hook or crook, an opportunity to amass wealth, and all this in the name of service of the people. A few even do not care if the interests of the country as a whole are jeopardized by their unscrupulous activities. It seems that there is unbridled freedom with which selfish ends are pursued. Also there are people who though free do not seem to find any way to get out from their misery. In this scenario most people do not see beyond their immediate interest, and seek to make best of the opportunity by the position they occupy anywhere in the system whether placed in a lower cadre or in the higher one. Thus freedom remains either unrealized or is being misused without scruples.

It seems that the malaise is not merely contemporary though its extent may have varied from age to age. In India it must have existed in ancient times also for otherwise how the ancient wise people could advise people not to neglect *dharma,* that is, duty, self-control and justice. They recognized *'artha'* and *'kama'* as *'purusarthas* – the worthy objects to be pursued' but they insisted that they should be regulated by *'dharma'* - they had to be *'dharmaviruddha'* – not contrary to *dharma.* Such a code of conduct could be followed only if individuals realized the true significance of their freedom. Since they are free they could move in the direction of evil or good. Nobody could doubt in what direction one should move. Of course, there are problems when one has to decide what is good and right

While it is clear to see in most cases what is evil, it is difficult to decide what is good. And sometime the misunderstanding of what is good leads the doer towards evil. Those who emphasized that one should follow dharma, also recommended that one should follow 'swadharma' which was understood as the place one occupied in the society. The kind of society the ancient Aryans visualized was divided into well known four classes – *bhrahmana, kshatriyas, vaishyas* and *sudras.* The division was based on the function that the member of each class had to perform. The manner in which *sudras* were treated was a degenerate form of manual worker and was the bane of fourfold division. However, the core idea underlying the notion of *'swadharma'* could be spelled out in terms of one's duty as a human being, as a member of a family, as a member of society, as a functionary and so on. *'Kama'* as desire cannot be wished away. Desire is presupposed in action. *Artha* is that towards which the action is directed, what one wants to achieve, attain or possess. It is necessary as a support for living, and living well. But duty has an overriding place. One is supposed to see that the fulfillment of desires does not trespass a certain limit and does not lead to the neglect of duty. The feeling that one's actions do not cause any harm or injury to others is the best guard against the trespass of duty. One has to realize that one's freedom requires the recognition of the freedom of the other. The notion of freedom must be compatible with the notion of the freedom of the other.

Sometimes there is serious conflict between the loyalty to a group and what dictates of reason or conscience command. Since an individual is a member of some group or the other such a situation is likely to be encountered if the individual exercises her or his reason and judgement. The situation becomes much more severe and difficult when it is realized that an individual can be a member of more than one group. How to steer clear through the demands of conformity and freedom? Several things may happen. The individual may opt out of the membership of the group. Alternatively, s/he may be turned out of the group. If the number of members whose dissent is sizable the group may break into more groups or may remain enmeshed in internal conflicts and tensions. Two remedial considerations suggest themselves in order that such a situation is not allowed to arise or if arisen then to overcome it. First there must be some mechanism within the structure of the group which allows the notice of dissent and an honest and open discussion about the issues dissenters raise. Secondly and perhaps, more important is the requirement that before voicing the dissent the individual has satisfied herself or himself that the dissent is in the interest of a larger good and is not merely motivated by one's narrow self interest. Unfortunately both these steps are usually neglected because of personal interests, prejudices and egoistic tendency of the members of the group.

Though dissent and resistance invite oppression and coercion they prove the fact that individuals are free to think and act. There is no doubt that one may have to pay huge price for one's freedom. On the other hand such struggles, in the long run, enhance the strength, insight and confidence of the individual, for the struggle is a fight for right and justice.

What we have been discussing so far has been concerned with freedom to do something. But freedom to do also requires freedom from something. If I am not free from certain preoccupations I may not have an opportunity to do something else. If I am not free from illness, from the worry for the next meal, from the assignment assigned to me by someone, I cannot do anything different. Let us say, there will be no opportunity to do what I wish to do. Possibility of opportunity or rather the utilizing the opportunity requires that there is space for me to act and pursue my objective.

Opportunities depend on the one hand on being free from certain conditions but on the other hand they also depend on the cognitive spread and imagination of an individual. What opportunities are there requires a good scanning of various alternatives available and this would depend in turn on what a person knows and how creative her or his imagination is. In other words our choices are not merely restricted by external circumstances and our own physical fitness but their extent is also determined by our knowledge and imagination. This consideration implies that our choices also depend on how we have formed ourselves. Thus basically the limitation of choices can ultimately be reduced, to a large extent, to our own efforts to develop ourselves which in turn would presuppose how self conscious we are about our aims and objectives that we wish to pursue in our lives.

There is, however, a skeptical and cynical view about the very nature of our worldly existence. According to this view existence is full of miseries and sufferings. Even the occasional pleasures are followed by all kinds of sufferings. Therefore, one must think how to get rid of suffering. But this is not possible, we are told, unless we are able to see through the reality of existence. When we try to find out whether there is any meaning in life or existence we find that there is none. Everything is transitory. Pleasure is momentary. It is no good to run after such transitory or momentary objects. We should seek happiness which never diminishes and which is always there. We cannot get such happiness from the transitory objects. In fact, the character of happiness is very different from worldly pleasures which always bring suffering in their trail. This view suggests that we should get freedom from desires. Desires enmesh us in external temptations and lead us astray. Attraction of external objects creates desire, so we should be aware of such a trap and get freedom from all desires.

We get entangled in the trap of desire because we confuse our self with our body. It is our body where desires originate. So far as our true self is concerned, it is neither a doer nor a consumer. Body belongs to the domain of three *gunas,* while self is beyond the three *gunas.* Desires, actions, pleasures and sufferings and all kind of changes describe the worldly existence which falls in the realm of *prakrti* – another name of the configuration of three *gunas.* Pure self has nothing to do with *prakrti.* This is the self which we have forgotten. Thus the real task is to get freedom from the desires and realize our true self. This self is pure happiness – *ananda.*

It is clear that such a 'freedom from' has little to do with 'freedom to do'. Such a view, obviously, is a negation of the world. But so long as we live or we have to live, we cannot survive with this negation. We have to act, perform activities essential for living, at the minimum. Transcendentalists recognize this fact and thus are compelled to propose a notion of a secondary existence which accommodates the world and whatever goes on in it. It is in this secondary existence or the world – *vyavaharajagat* or the phenomenal world, that whatever we have been talking about earlier would make any sense. Now, if we are compelled to live in the *vyavaharajagat* and we are advised to seek true knowledge of self and realize that self also, how these two objectives could be attained at the same time? We are being asked to get freedom from the world and we are also being asked to do our duties? How the two can go together?

One answer is proposed by *Gita*. We should renounce the thought of fruits of action and should be concerned ourselves only with doing our duties. Perhaps the idea is that once we have chosen our objective and the means to attain it we should forget what would be the results and devote ourselves wholly in performing our duty. But if this much is granted, then we are back in the world of change, desires, ends and all that follows. We may perform our duties as assigned to us or as we come to see them but we also act because there are desires, of course, they have to be legitimate, in our own interest as well as in the interest of larger good. Such a consideration implies an understanding of legitimacy, interest, and the larger good which in turn is not easy to come by in view of our finite situation on the one hand and the existence of other fellow beings on the other.

In sum it may be said that life implies action and action implies freedom to choose, decide and act. But freedom to think and act is possible only within certain conditions – physical and social. Unbridled freedom is no freedom. One cannot be free unless one has space for the freedom of the other.

Understanding and Dialogue

"To reach an understanding in a dialogue is not merely a matter of putting oneself forward and successfully asserting one's own point of view, but being transformed into a communion in which we do not remain what we were." Hans-Georg Gadamar.

'Well, I did not mean it', 'I did not mean to hurt you', 'you have not understood me' – these and similar expressions occur in our verbal interaction with the other person quiet frequently. One of the obvious points to notice when we think of such expressions is that we are often misunderstood. We are not the privileged ones in this respect. We too misunderstand the other person/s as often. When misunderstanding occurs, and there is lack of tolerance or concern on the part of one or both the interlocutors, the interaction may take up a bad turn. If the misunderstanding persists, and there is no will to reach at proper understanding, the interaction may lead to cessation of relationship. It may turn into a hostile relationship thereby resulting in certain very undesirable results. Fortunately in day to day cases, misunderstanding soon gets resolved and the matter ends there. Yet what does it mean to say that we understand and what happens when we misunderstand someone and how does that come about.

When we say, 'I did not mean it', we often rephrase what we wanted to say in order to be better understood and reach out the other person. (There may be other situations in which an expression of this kind may be used, for example, when somebody has committed some error or something wrong but for the time being let us consider the present situation.) In that case there occurs a willingness to continue the dialogue and arrive at a proper understanding. There is an effort not to let the relationship be damaged. It is not merely rephrasing the expression, but the effort to reach out and make a successful communication, which may affect our gestures, our tone, in short our body language. All these factors combined may result into a successful communication. But this is only a part of the story. The success of the communication would also depend on the person who listens to us or to whom we address. She or he may not be in a mood to listen to us at all. Or may have prejudged the issue as a consequence of which one may not properly listen to what we say, or may interpret what I say into the meanings consonant with one's pre-judged opinion. In such a case the communication may break down.

Thus it would require that both the interlocutors are sincerely moved to communicate with each other, and have a genuine motivation to understand each other. In such a case, even an improper or unsuitable expression, or mispronounced word, would make no difference. If there are no preconceptions or prejudices and relationship is amicable, the right message gets across somehow. The fact that two persons have an amicable disposition towards each other facilitates communication. Thus amongst the various conditions attending a communicative interaction, the condition of the mode of a prior relationship between two persons becomes quite significant. So far, what we are talking about has to do with familiar and positive ambience. The persons are known to each other, perhaps they may have been living with each other for some time and in the same house or working in the same institution, they may belong to the same culture, may be using the same language – thus having several features common between them. Above all there is a sincere desire on both sides to understand each other.

But there may be situations in which these features may be absent – some or all. In other words the persons may be strangers to each other. They may have a common language and may be living in the same city. Suppose two strangers having an encounter in a journey. May be they start talking to each other beginning with how fine the weather is or some such thing. In such a case the talk might take the form of mutual exploration. It often happens that the two persons after a while are exchanging their views in such a way as if they knew each other for quite a long time. They might note down each other's addresses or phone numbers with a view to renew the relationship at a later date, after the journey is over.

The interesting thing about such an interaction is that there are no pre-existing images in the psychic make up of the two persons, since they began as being complete strangers to each other. Perhaps there also exists no axe to grind and so the talk is not motivated by any specific self interest.

Being exploratory the interaction becomes interesting for its own sake. In fact, it is closer to the type of discussions which take place in a seminar around a table amongst the delegates coming from different backgrounds. There would be, however, a major difference between the two cases. The discussion in a seminar would be around some specific themes and much more systematic and directed.

The cases we have considered indicate various features involved in the communicative interaction. The accidental encounters or familiar interactions, both provide a suitable stage for a communicative interaction provided the persons concerned have no negative images of each other, are not prejudiced, are free from mutual ill will and have a sincere desire to communicate. In such cases, the attempt to understand each other is highly motivated and backed by innocent inquisitiveness. Unfortunately this does not happen when the individuals are known to each other before hand and have already prejudged images of each other. And, as we noticed, the matter turns out to be worse, if the images are negative. Negative images may be formed because of direct contact resulting in some unhappy situation or in an indirect way through hearsay. There may have been unhappy situations that such images are formed.

Anthropologists try to understand primitive cultures and try to reach out to tribal people. When entering in an area in which some tribe has its habitat, investigators have to move with several precautions. The most important thing is that they should see that their moves do not create any panic or scare amongst members of the tribal community.

Their efforts have to be such that they are able to establish a rapport with the members of the community in the first instance. This of course, is a difficult exercise, particularly in the absence of knowledge of the language and the semantic significance of the gestures of those peoples. Once they are able to establish a rapport with those people, they gradually acquire the understanding of their language and meanings of their gestures and movements also. And that is the beginning of the long travail of understanding a strange people. The importance of keeping an open mind, coupled with a friendly and warm disposition towards these strangers and treating them as equals permits mutual understanding. A prior amount of information in respect of the tribe should come as a help.

Such an attitude and approach play an important role when one accosts with members of an alien culture. From the very early times, some adventurous people were making attempt to move out of their own country and venture into the alien lands, for purposes of trade and commerce, knowledge and learning. Besides commerce and knowledge, victors taking possession of those they have defeated, had to learn their language and culture in order to control them in a better way. We are living in times when it is possible to learn about the language, culture and climate of the other country before venturing into a travel into that country. Better the understanding of the alien people better the possibility of having successful deals with them. The sheer fact of mutually being strange to each other, sometimes, generates a tolerant attitude towards the other, provided there is a will to understand.

Paradoxically, the problems of understanding abound when it comes to relationships which are rather close as compared to the relationships with strangers. Sometimes that happens in respect of those people who have been living together for quite some time and are, for all apparent purpose, well known to each other. The classical example of generation gap comes to mind. Parents fail to understand their children and children fail to understand their parents. Such a situation presents a rich case for understanding the shift of interests, values and attitudes in a micro realm. Parents are forced to be reflective about their habitual beliefs and children have to develop some empathy with their parents. Perhaps the use of the term 'children' is inappropriate here for we are thinking of the children who are grown up and have already developed their own ways of thinking.

Divorces provide examples of estrangement within close relationships as a consequence of break-down of mutual understanding and tolerance. Whether it is in respect of the relationship between the spouses or the relationship between the elders and younger people, it seems that matters other than the 'concern for the other' acquire greater force and affect the manner of thinking and behaviour of people. It appears that there is an unwillingness to understand the other person. Ego becomes more dominant. Sometimes narrow interests, or undue expectations or emotional imbalance generate conflict and hostility. Reason, sympathy and concern for the other take back seats.

These factors indicate that the fact of strangeness, ignorance of language and ways of living, do not present hurdles great enough to disturb the process of mutual understanding as do the narrow self interests, immediate concerns, ignoring remote consequences, disregarding pain and feeling of the other and an exaggerated feeling of 'I-ness' and 'my interest'. Once the understanding breaks down, relationships are damaged and family or friendship breaks down. Similar phenomenon occurs when we think of an encounter of a member of one community with the member of the other community. People of different communities living in the same locality or city for a long time are suddenly found to be violently hostile to each other. The narrow interests or vested interests which lead to such violent encounters may or may not have their origin within the communities or outside them. Communal conflicts often turn out to be generated owing to misinformation, political interests, misunderstanding of religious heritage and sometime because of a hope to gain out of the fray.

Understanding becomes oppressive when the relationship between two individuals is asymmetric. Relationships between superior and subordinate, master and slave, victor and vanquished, father and son, teacher and taught, husband and wife exhibit asymmetric relationships. In such cases, the junior is supposed to listen and accept the command or advice and not to question it. When action is a necessity, decision has to be quick, no leisure to think or deliberate, the advice or the command has to be carried out. However, it may also be possible that there is something radically wrong in the command and too obvious to be ignored. In such a case, if the command is carried out, the consequences may turn out to be disastrous. One is reminded of the well known poem of Tennyson - Charge the Light Brigade. (This is a poem in which, the poet has raised the obedience of the soldiers in terms of great valour and the sense of duty, even though the command given to them had been based on a misunderstanding). On the other hand if the command is not obeyed then the system or the organization is likely to break down. Dissent and revolt are natural consequences of a flawed command. There are, of course, many other factors which lead to dissent or revolt such as exploitation, corruption, mismanagement and so on. This obviously enhances the responsibility of those in command; they must understand the situation and the reasonableness of their command before issuing a command.

It is now generally believed that such a situation is not conducive to dedicated, efficient and innovative effort. As a result the necessity and importance of making the other person understand with reasons what is desired or what is to be done have come to be emphasized. One - way communication is to be pushed aside. Ideas and suggestions are solicited even from the younger people who may be in the position of junior or subordinate assistants but such a practice is not widespread yet.

In the context of family, the relationship between elders and the younger ones on the one hand and the spouses on the other is of crucial importance. If members of the family are not attuned to each other, the spillover is neither good for the family nor for the society. Thus the significance of mutual understanding and smooth communication amongst the members of a family for the attunement and harmony within the family cannot be overemphasized. A family can be looked at as a conveyer of the culture within which it is placed. To a large extent it inherits the cultural constraints and conventions though mostly in an informal way. It maintains and sustains the cultural values either consciously or unconsciously. Blind adherence to such values and not realizing the demands of the changing times and consequent changing needs often clash with each other and often generate tension and conflicts in the family. This places a great responsibility on the elders of the family. They need to examine their beliefs and be sensitive to the emerging needs of the younger generation. But this presupposes that members of a family feel the need to examine and reflect on relationships involved.

The cultural configuration of a family is determined by that segment of society to which it belongs. As is well known Hindu society is divided in a broad way by the varna system and at a more specific level by caste system. The levels of economic or financial well being further determine the status of a family. Obviously this applies to families irrespective to which country or culture they belong. Divisions also exist in other communities which are determined both by their cultural demands as well as by the financial status. A further impact can be traced to the shift which their origins have experienced by way of religious conversion. The details of these features belong to anthropological and sociological investigation. In the present context, we need merely keep this in our mind that the relationships in any family between the various members are largely determined by their cultural heritage, contemporary pressures and also by the individual temperaments.

But the heritage does not remain well formed and static. As we noticed, changes in times slow or fast, sooner or later introduce demands on the members for which they are often not prepared. Increase in the number of members in the family, location of employment or occupations at a distant place, the uneven occupation and financial resources of different members of the family – all these features are sometime at odd with the traditional values of the family. Besides, there are pressures to maintain a certain standard, a place and identity in the society which is often determined by financial or positional status. Add to the complexity the temperamental differences of different members and their own interests and ambitions which may often be at cross purposes with each other.

Now it is within such a scenario that one has to think of the mutual understanding amongst the various members of a family. Obviously, the major responsibility of understanding the situation within which the family is placed, the demands and pressures it has to meet, the growth and career of the young ones, lies on the elders of the family. If the elders are not able to maintain a proper approach to the right kind of values, which may not be the ones which they have inherited and which require modification or replacement in the light of new demands which the present stringencies call for, if they remain indifferent to the capabilities, interests and ambitions of the young ones, if they remain occupied with their own interests and projects to the neglect of the other members of the family, then tensions are bound to be generated in the family. These tensions may partially or totally disturb the attunement and harmony of the family.

If everybody is concerned with one's own interest and projects being indifferent to the interest and projects of the other person, possibility of a dialogue or understanding would decrease. One serious problem with the elders of a family has to do with the regard that they have towards themselves. They are conscious of the fact that they are elders. This alone makes them think that they are entitled to unquestioned obedience. What they think or decide is right and proper just because it is what they think or decide, for they are the elder ones. Since they are the elder ones they know better what is good or bad and what is right and wrong. Cool and objective reasons may or may not enter into their deliberation. It is clear that such an attitude may elicit obedience only if the position is also accompanied with sound financial position and a certain status in the society. Yet, it may happen that the young ones may refuse to accept the situation as it is and may start resisting and finally defying the authority which the elders wish to exercise.

It is here that the idea of generation gap becomes operative. The perception, understanding, thoughts and beliefs of the young ones may be radically different from those of their elders. Consequently they may not think with their elders eye to eye. Such a situation presents a challenge to all concerned so far understanding each other is concerned. As already noted, a will to understand coupled with patience and an attempt to empathize is essential to meet such a challenge. It seems to be natural to expect the elders to initiate the process because of the simple fact that they are elders and thus more responsible with their long experience.

So far as the upper middle class and higher echelons of the society are concerned more permissiveness and a disregard of the sanctity of family ties and of wedlock seem to be increasing. Even the judiciary (in India) has approved the companionship of man and woman without a wedding as legal. The structure of family as it obtained earlier is bound to become radically different. It seems that the cementing force of a family that is the existence of a child is no more central to the relationship between man and woman as it is gradually coming to prevail. The companionship may get stronger and lasting but it may also become a matter of convenience and may break down on very trivial grounds or for no reason at all.

In fact, such a situation may reduce the necessity of understanding and dialogue, for the relationship would remain loose right from the beginning and the members in the relationship may not be very serious about its continuity. The worth and dignity of the person may not remain as important as certain experiences or benefits resulting out of the relationship. In that case the other may not be more important than being a means to the fulfillment of an end. The facts of life as can be detected from around the world seem to support such apprehensions. It seems to be obvious that such a life would be poorer, lonely and more boring than what it would be otherwise.

These considerations become more worrying when it is realized that family provides not only a basic unit of structure of the society, but it is also a source of all worth-while values which enrich life. It is an arena within which crucial experiments are performed in human living. It would not be an exaggeration to say that the mode and quality of society reflects ultimately the mode and quality of its basic unit – the family. The family reflects almost all those features which characterize a society in its larger frame. In a family there are young and old, there are men and women, there are individuals growing up and there are individuals grown up, there are illiterate and unskilled members – very young ones, and there are literate and skilled ones, there are sick ones and there are healthy ones, there are members who have less control on what goes on around them while there are others who have greater control on the affairs of the family. Different members have different sort of desires, different sort of projects and designs. Differences in the thinking of different members also characterize a family.

The needs and activities of the family lead to the various aspects of a society – religious, cultural, social, economic and political. The problems which arise in a family as a consequence of there being different types of members also arise in the society in its larger frame. Thus the challenge to understanding and dialogue become central to family as well as the society. Since two persons differ from each other, necessity for understanding each other becomes of crucial significance. The dispositional characteristics essential for proper understanding and dialogue are not only instrumental in solving difficult problems but they also enrich human personalities in so far as they help in the growth of positive and constructive potentials of human nature.

Concern for the other, regard for the other as a person as oneself, a will to understand, and to be able to see the point of view of the other from the point of the other herself or himself are dispositional features which can provide supports to keep the family intact as well as the society of which the family constitutes a basic unit. It might appear that this goody good talk ignores certain very basic issues which create problems for living together. For example, if two persons are diametrically opposed in their thinking, have opposed sets of beliefs, have had different kind of experiences, and consequently have different plans of life, how can there be a dialogue between them. How can they be brought to the same table to talk to each other? What role can understanding have in such a conflicting situation when it seems to characterize major contexts of contemporary life?

This should also be kept in mind that most human beings are mainly propelled by their immediate concerns and projects. These concerns and projects do not permit them to have any regard for the other unless the other may happen to facilitate their designs. Such a thing is true at the level of the individual, at the level of family, at the level of society and also at the level of nation or country. That is why we have any number of problems afflicting our social and national life. Once again, it is in the family that human beings learn to live with each other. The hope for a better world has its source in the success which one attains in the experiment of living with one another for which family provides ample opportunities.

Verbal exchanges in one direction are more frequent then dialogue. Requests, commands, advices are generally expressed without expecting any negative response. There are occasions when they are resisted or disobeyed. In such cases a verbal altercation may take place. It may or may not be in the form of a dialogue. The dialogue suggests a situation in which two persons try to understand each other and respond accordingly. One wishes that such a thing happened more frequently. Unfortunately what happens is quite different. There seems to be a strong desire on the part of the speaker to have his full say and prevail upon the interlocutor. Sometime the person tries to say or tell or to communicate something which s/he thinks to be important, but there are times when the speakers seem to say something to communicate, but in fact, s/he expresses her or his feelings or emotions without being conscious that s/he is not actually trying to convey some message but is merely expressing herself or himself. The other person often fails to grasp this fact and takes the harangue as directed to her or him, gets worked up and starts speaking in the same vein. The consequence is that both the persons express their feelings misunderstanding each other though they seem to be addressing each other. The verbal exchange instead of being a dialogue becomes a verbal combat.

Elders have to control their resentment or irritation and young ones have to be more patient. If equals are involved they have to be more patient and understanding towards each other. It may be asked as to what extent fairness and reasoning enter into such exchanges. First thing to note is that fairness and reasoning would have their place only if the parties engaged have self control, composure and an open mind. Each allows the other enough opportunity to express one's problem or point of view. However, self-control, composure and an open mind do not present themselves in ready manner. One has to attain these dispositional characteristics through a long conscious effort. Once again the matter has to begin with the elders. They have to look to themselves, introspect, and self reflect. They have also to realize that the kind of responses they receive from the younger members, are to a great extent a result of their own training and bringing up or lack of them.

These demands arise because elders do not do what they ought to be doing. It has also to be noted that realizing self-awareness or self- reflection is not something which just happens without any effort. Mostly ad hoc solutions are sought. Little thought is given to remote consequences. When traumatic situations arise then there are attempts to abdicate responsibility and shift the burden of undesirable consequences on others or extraneous circumstances. Fortunately each of us is endowed with a self-corrective mechanism which forces us to think more seriously and deeply about the situation we have to face.

As already noted, to be able to think about any issue properly or in the right way it is necessary to keep mind open. In order to do that it is necessary that for a while we keep our prejudices, preoccupations and interests in the background.

The most important thing is not to fall prey to snares of ego. This effort is one side of the coin. The other side is a concern for the other – other as being on the same pedestal as oneself and having the same worth as oneself. These are the conditions which enable us to understand – understand a person, understand an expression, understand a text and understand a given situation. A proper understanding backs a proper action. A proper action is likely to make this world a better world. Living together is the most venturesome experiment. Understanding, dialogue and successful communication are central to this experiment. Love of truth and rational approach on the one hand and certain positive dispositional qualities on the other, and the concern and regard for the other make understanding possible.

There is an interesting dialogue which took place between Menander a Greek king who reigned in the North West of India about five hundred years after Buddha and a Buddhist monk called Nagsena. The text where the dialogue can be found is called Milinda (Menander) Prasna. This text contains many such dialogues which centre on the various ideas of Buddhism.

The king said: 'Reverend Sir, will you discuss with me?'

'If your Majesty will discuss as a scholar (pandit), well; but if you will discuss as a king, no.'

'How is it then that scholars discuss?'

'When scholars talk a matter over one with another then is there a winding up, and an unravelling; one or other is convicted of error, and he then acknowledges his mistake; distinctions are drawn, and contra-distinctions; and yet thereby they are not angered. Thus do scholars, O king, discuss.'

'And how do kings discuss?'

'When a king, your Majesty, discusses a matter, and he advances a point, if any one differ from him on that point, he is apt to fine him, saying: "Inflict such and such a punishment upon that fellow!" Thus, your Majesty, do kings discuss.'

'Very well. It is as a scholar, not as a king, that I will discuss. Let your reverence talk unrestrainedly, as you would with a brother, or a novice, or a lay disciple, or even with a servant. Be not afraid!'

'Very good, your Majesty,' said Nâgasena, (*Milindapannah,* translated. In Hindi by Bhikkhu Jagdish Kashyap, Samyak Prakashan, New Delhi. Pp 56-57)

Notice that Nagsena agrees to converse only when the king promises that he would not act like a king but like another scholar. Also see how Nagsena describes a dialogue between two scholars.

Suffering and Happiness

"Bhikkhuo, It is a noble truth that suffering can be eliminated. Complete elimination of craving, its abnegation, its complete annihilation, results into a detached thoughtless state. And that is release." Gautam Buddha.

Most sensitive and thoughtful people have found this world and living in it highly dissatisfactory. They have found human existence full of suffering both in physical as well as in mental sense. A large number of people work very hard for their living and yet do not get even the minimum to survive in a satisfactory way. Many need shelter, food, clothing and sanitary facilities. On the other hand, a minority of people lives a life of blinding affluence. These are not stable and static classes including the middle one, yet the social mobility is not fast. It some time happens that a rich person meets misfortune and looses whatever he had. And similarly, this also happens that man in penury has risen to the status of a very affluent person. But these are accidents or exceptions

Not all people who are affluent are affluent because of their accomplishments and similarly not all those who are poor are poor because they have done something to deserve their fate. Thus in many cases there appears to be no relationship in what people do and what they gain or suffer. Their affluence or poverty is a consequence of descent and inheritance. Those who think that there is definite relationship between what people do and what they get have to account for such exceptions in various ways. In our country, amongst Hindus, one of the main reasons given is in terms of the actions of the past life. People with theological bent and having different beliefs about after-life might sometimes say that misfortunes are meant to test the steadfastness of the adherent. Still others might think that one should wait for the better results, for some times good deeds do not result in appropriate fruits immediately. Or that there must be something good which remains hidden to us but which we may attain at some later date. It is also said that lesser misfortune or evil displaces larger misfortune.

There is a radically different approach according to which relationship between the deed and the results are not to be seen in a necessary or definite way. In fact the relationship is contingent and depends on several other conditions which are determined by the structure and organization of the social network itself. In a structure or organization based on usually far from just or satisfactory in case of the majority of people. As the suffering class of people realizes that it is the other class of better placed people that is responsible for their misery and poor state and this class is not going to settle for proper distribution of resources willingly, they may wage a war against this class. Such a struggle would introduce in the system violence and may cause disruptions which may not result into the desired results immediately.

People may have to wage a long and costly war in order to have the system changed.

It should be noted that the motivation and logistics of all the members of a warring group are not homogenous. Sincerity, freedom from narrow self-interest and lack of opportunism are not always forthcoming. Consequently the struggle often gets diffused or turns into mindless assaults. The indifference and callousness of the privileged and ruling class which refuses to recognize the right of the downtrodden to a dignified life worsens the situation. In the name of public interest and development, projects are adopted which involve displacement of large populations without proper rehabilitation. In the implementation of most schemes an opportunist and corrupt segment soaks away the allocations and a meager amount reaches the beneficiaries if at all. What is being witnessed as terrorism in its various forms can partly be seen as a consequence of such a mismatch.

Thus there are two ways in which human misfortune and suffering can be viewed. First in the light of a just cosmic order, it is believed that according to such an order right and good actions are appropriately rewarded, and bad and evil actions result into punishment and misfortune. Either there is no departure from such rule, or if there is an apparent case which seems to be a deviation then accounts have been supplied to explain why such a thing happens. According to the other way of thinking there ought to be a proper social order which is based on justice, equality and freedom, which actually does not obtain in reality. It is because of the dissatisfactory state of the social organization itself that a large number of people suffer.

There is yet another consideration which once again takes us back to the notion of the cosmic order. Think of the natural calamities, such as earth quake, volcanic eruption, tsunami, landslides, avalanches, cyclones and tornadoes and epidemics and accidents owing to human or non-human cause/s. There has been a belief that if the king or the ruler does not perform his duty the way he ought, and people live a life of sin and evil, then a natural calamity is a way to punish all concerned. Proper living of people and right governance of the ruler are accompanied with good harvest. These beliefs imply several important considerations. The state is properly governed, people are allowed and facilitated in performing their duties, people do sincerely perform their duties, there is attunement with nature in the sense that the eco-balance is maintained, if we take from nature then we have some obligation towards nature also – these are the things which are inter connected. Neglect or indifference judge and enforcing order in human affairs may not be accepted as a rational thesis, yet it can not be gainsaid that there is a close relationship between what human beings do and what happens in nature. The increasing awareness regarding the nature of consumption and global warming points in that direction.

The concepts of governance, duty and obligation, and due regard for nature imply that ultimately it is human thinking and human behaviour which underlie any human project. An organization or an institution is a human product, that is, it is result of collective thinking and action. What form an organization or an institution would be there, how it would be maintained and sustained would ultimately depend on the attitude and concern of its members. A system is run according to certain rules. The content of these rules and their orientation shapes the system and its progress. But if certain behavioural rules are not observed, are not taken seriously and sincerely, then no system can run.

In *Gautam Sutra* – a *smriti* text which describes and prescribes rules of behaviour, certain sacraments or samskaras are supposed to organize and lend orientation to human activities. These sacraments are supposed to be forty in number which include some to be performed at the time of birth, at the time of beginning of the education, at the time of marriage and so forth. Apart from these sacraments some guide lines for behaviour are also mentioned. In fact they are understood as the attributes of a worthy individual. These are – to be compassionate towards all the living beings, to be forgiving and tolerant, not to be envious of the progress of the other, to be clean and pure, to do well without, not to beg, and remain distant from greed. The important thing we are told is that if all the sacraments are observed but these dispositional qualities are not cultivated then the individual cannot attain Brahmaloka – the state of summum bonum, and one who is shorn of the sacraments but who has these dispositional qualities, then he is entitled to attain Brahmaloka. (1.8, 24-26)

This text is very ancient and it is amazing that the seer had seen the crucial need of the discipline of the individual if any social project were to succeed. Without minimizing the need of a proper structure of social organization and good governance, the necessity to cultivate a race of people with intrinsic worthy dispositional attributes cannot be over emphasized. That everyone in a society would have proper disposition, everyone would discharge her or his duty, everyone would show mutual concern and regard for one another – this is to expect a utopia. Society is a dynamic system. New elements enter into it and old ones disappear. Each fresh entrant would require to train or discipline herself or himself. That is why a social organization needs an educational system. Because of the fact that each individual attempts to develop herself or himself and remains in a process of continuous growth and development, one may be subject to deviations, deficiencies, and defects – moral and mechanical also. In the process of development one has to keep an eye on these and has to constantly struggle to win them over.

Failure to win them over or submitting to them would bring in disorder, injustice, misery, pain and suffering. Each of us passively or actively, consciously or unconsciously contributes to these conditions, if we do not live reflectively. Unless we reflect on what we think and what we do with a view to larger concerns, and we remain confined to our immediate projects and prospects without thinking of the remote consequences, we are likely to add to the chaos which in its turn is going to be unbearable for us. We have been talking about sufferings and misfortunes but it may be asked what is meant by them.

Who does not know the well known story about the famous prince of Kapilvastu. For the first time when he encountered a sick man, an old man and a dead man, he was struck by the sorrows awaiting anyone who lives. For him sickness, old age and death were the sorrows that afflict a living being and there is no escape from them. The pain one undergoes while sick, the infirmities one suffers while old and the anxiety about death, are enough to fill in life with sufferings. The severity of these sufferings would increase according to the extent of deprivations one suffers. In another major stream of Indian thinking, that is, Samkhya system, three types of suffering are mentioned – *adhyatmika, adhibhautika* and *adhidaivika*. These are sufferings owing to the diseases of the body, sufferings due to the parting or near or dear ones, sufferings resulting from attacks from men, animals, birds or snakes etc, and sufferings caused by the natural happenings such as excessive rain and so on. In all these cases suffering is something happening to us because of something on which we do not seem to have any control. In other words, we neither invited them nor we did something to deserve them.

Often we blame others for our sufferings. They have not cared for us. They have deceived us. They have been unfaithful to us. They have stabbed us in our back. They have exploited us. They have tortured us. And so on. In all this we are not at all aware of our own role. While this is true that we are often made victim because of others' malicious interests, designs and actions. Others may be jealous of our prosperity or they may feel superior to us and expect from us obedience. But this is also true that we too are afflicted with the same sort of defects of dispositions as others are. Either we are not conscious of how we speak to others or behave with them, or if we are, then we find reasons for our misconduct. Such a thing comes to pass because there is either lack of mutual understanding or there is positive desire to exploit the other and above all an absence of self-reflection.

This cannot be gainsaid that many sufferings are due to an unamiable relationship which in turn may be due to immaturity, lack of proper attitude, an evil desire to hurt or cheat and so on. Thus for such suffering we human beings ourselves are responsible. A group of people can function harmoniously only if each member of the group is sincere about her or his role and duties in the group. Unfortunately such a harmony is rare. Although it is a difficult exercise, yet a patient, compassionate, and understanding approach can improve the existing relationship a long way.

Pain, suffering and misfortunes ought to be distinguished from each other. Pain is physical, it hurts somewhere in the body. Suffering is a mental uneasiness or discomfort. Misfortune is loosing ones possessions or near or dear ones. Since conscious feeling accompany each of these it may be said that basically it is the conscious uneasiness and discomfort which constitutes suffering. People may put up with misfortunes and even tolerate intense pain, if they have a courageous, enduring, and a large-hearted attitude and disposition. Such a stoic temperament presupposes an understanding of the nature of existence and our place in it. There are things and events which happen without our volition or intervention. We have to watch and face them. There are things which are of our own making and if we have the will, we can do something about them and have the situation improved. There are things which have to do with the system – generally bad, deficient and discrepant, to which we belong and it requires the understanding of the dynamics of the system on the one hand and carefully planned strategy to correct it on the other. This obviously involves long struggle for it goes against the vested interests of those who are responsible for the ills of the society.

It is in contrast to suffering that we think of happiness or joy. Happiness and joy can be distinguished from pleasure, though the term 'pleasure' sometime used in a wide sense. Generally pleasure has to do with some kind of bodily fulfillment or satisfaction. Rather, we should say enjoyment in which bodily needs are met. To be in a comfortable state, to have tasteful things to consume, to behold things or persons who are beautiful, to listen to melodious and harmonious sounds, to be amidst peaceful, exhilarating, and serene surroundings – all these indicate various kinds of pleasures which most of us would aspire to enjoy, if possible. Alternatively there is a calm and serene state of mind, in which we are not aware of any specific demand or seek any external object, but in which we feel at peace with ourselves and seem to desire nothing. Such a state of awareness may be called the state of happiness or a state close to it.

Thus there is a fulfillment or satisfaction which we have when we are able to consume some object, or be able to possess it, or be in its company or in the company of a person whom we like or love. Obviously such a fulfillment or satisfaction takes us away from ourselves. We are bound to be uncomfortable, uneasy and in pain, if we are not able to fulfill our desire. On the other hand, in the state of desirelessness, when we are left to ourselves, and we do not depend on anything such as some object or some person, we may be said to be happy. Advaita Vedantins hold that the highest stage of awareness is really the awareness of pure consciousness, pure in the sense, that there is no object to occupy it, and it is such awareness which is one with happiness. For the Vedantins truth, happiness or bliss and pure consciousness are same.

The awareness which does not require an external object, nor does it require even any internal object in the sense of some pleasant memory, does not lead to any activity. Nor any action can lead to it. Action is normally associated with an effort to obtain something, or to make something, or to modify or improve something. It may even be destructive, for sometime in order to make something new you have to destroy something old or you have to reduce a whole to pieces in order to re-arrange it into a new pattern and so on. But if the destination is objectless consciousness, action is redundant.

There are experiences which involve some object and yet do not require any advance towards an object in the sense that one is required to move towards an external object to obtain it or to bring about some change in the state of affairs or to create something. Aesthetic experiences are such experiences. A real aesthetic experience is rare to come by. We see paintings, sculptures, monuments, architectural wonders, a beautiful person, or any other beautiful thing or artifact, hear or read music or poetry and may like them, be provoked by them, or be amazed by them and so on. But there are occasion when we are lost in them. In such a state of mind the duality of subject and object disappears. In fiction, in poems of the size of epics or even long poems and other modes of literature, complete identity between subject and object is, generally not attained. In fact, a good piece of literature is likely to provoke or disturb the mind in an unusual manner. One is likely to be affected by such a piece to an extent as to have one's whole outlook changed and a radical change may be brought about in one's style of life. It is said that Gandhi read Ruskin's *Unto The Last* in one go while traveling. The book had tremendous impact on him. Similarly we learn about Immanuel Kant who when going through Rousseau's *Emile,* postponed his regular activities.

In aesthetics it is the non-dual state which marks the acme of aesthetic experience. Some things similar also happen in a sincere, dedicated and surrender to some deity. We generally call such an attitude an attitude of *bhakti* or devotion. Like aesthetic experience *bhakti* is also a rare experience. One can find devotees without number, but a real devotee would be hard to come by. In the aesthetic experience the object occupies the space of awareness in such a way that the feeling of 'I-ness' is almost absent. In bhakti too, the presence of deity occupies the consciousness of the devotee to such an extent that the devotee completely forgets oneself. The story begins in duality and ends in non-duality.

These brief narratives of prized states of mind or consciousness indicate the various modes in which one may be supposed to have true joy or happiness. The most significant thing to note is that either the duality of subject and object disappears in such experiences or the consciousness is completely object-less. In the kind of life we remain engrossed in our day today routine such experiences remain rare lights far away. These rich experiences are hard to possess. One can not remain with them for a long time. They may, of course, be more frequent in the life of some lucky one.

There are yet other experiences which though do not require a non-duality between the subject and the object, yet in which the object because of some peculiarity attracts our attention beyond measure. While speaking of the presence of God, Kant mentioned of morality within and starry heaven above. The amazing experiences which the modern astro-physicists and space scientists and those who study the secrets of the particles have are such and they are quite frequent. When one stands near the shores of a sea or ocean, or is able to watch high cliffs covered with snow, or the drops of the dew on a leaf in the morning, or dull dry leaves near the foot of some tall tree in a jungle, or the smile of a baby or of an old person having a face full of wrinkles, or the vast expanses of sand dunes, or the tears in the eyes of recently wed daughter leaving for her new home, - these and such other innumerable experiences touch you to the core of your being.

Whether they are aesthetic experiences, or the experiences of devotion, or the experiences of extra-ordinary aspects of ordinary beings or events, or gigantic phenomena, they are all experiences which are an end into themselves. They are not associated with any material utility, or possessive desire, or purposeful activity. One can be with them. One cannot possess them. One can enjoy them, one cannot consume them. All of them point to some mode of well-being, when the individual is at peace with oneself, when nothing more is desired or needed and nothing remains to do.

This is true that there is lot of pain and suffering in the life and in the world. But there are other type of experiences also which provide fullness to life. These experiences do not require any special kind of effort to enjoy them. They cannot be bought. They cannot be possessed. Anyone, with the normal human sensitiveness, can have them, enjoy them and be amazed by them.

In contrast, the charm of eternal happiness as the summum bonum of human existence has been having tremendous appeal as one finds from the religious cum spiritual texts, as well as from the speeches of the god-men all over. Let us remind ourselves for a while that the eternal happiness is supposed to be a state of pure consciousness which is free from the occupation of all kinds of objects – external or internal. As is well known, the treatise on Yoga by Patanjali recommends a whole gradual course involving concentration which ultimately leads to such a state. It is quite possible that some persons could have succeeded in attaining such a state and may be enjoying happiness. But for the people at large such a state of mind in which one would stay all along, does not seem to be easy to attain.

Concentration without there being present an object to consciousness would be a difficult exercise. But that does not mean that it would be impossible. The day to day pressures of life are such that even if one is able to attain such a state of consciousness for a while one can not stay in that state for long. Thus the concept of eternal happiness seems to be more of an ideal than what is really possible for a lay man. There is another important aspect which draws our attention. The ideal of eternal happiness is basically an ideal confined to some individual alone. It is close to the concept of liberation or salvation or *moksa*. Theoretically, such an ideal implies a 'no' to the world, and the concerns related to it. Swami Vivekananda had been critical of such an individual enterprise dissociated from all concern for the other. For him the essence of spiritualism lied in the active concern for our fellow beings particularly those who need help.

But is the ideal of happiness and no attachment with the things of the world are compatible with the requirement of doing duty or helping others are mutually? Or the question may be put in a different way. If I am mainly occupied with my own limited concerns without having regard for the other, or even about the remote consequences of my action, and I keep on worrying all the time about the possible outcome of my action, would it be possible for me to carry through my action to attain its objective? It must be the experience of most of us that the emotional anxiety about the outcome of the action interferes with the process of action and thereby might even abrogate the action. This shows that even in our day to day routine what we do or try to attain would be done with more efficiency and success if we perform our action without being emotionally worried about the outcome. Still better strategy would be that we reflect about the remote consequences of our action before deciding to do it. Such a reflection would lead us to the idea of inter-connection and the net-work within which we are placed and consequently to the favourable or adverse results which may recoil on us as a result of our proposed action.

Such an approach would involve us in the wider concerns and would allow us to view our actions and behaviour in a broader perspective. Such a perspective is not oblivious of our immediate needs but allows us to assess them in a proper way. We realize that our good or our welfare is linked with the good and the welfare of other people. We need both detachment and attachment on the one hand, and interest and disinterest on the other. Or, in other words, we need detached attachment or disinterested interest. This has been the main teaching of *Gita*. It might be asked how this is possible? Are we not trapped in contradictions?

It would appear that our desires impel us to attach ourselves to certain objects in such a way that it appears to us that our whole life is at stake if a desire is not fulfilled. In the immediacy of feeling the attachment to the object increases many fold. However, if we could some how bring us to reflect on the matter, delay the fulfillment of the desire we might be able to see that the object really is not that important for us.

Or we might come to think of an alternative which presents a better prospect. Such reflection gradually allows us to realize our needs in a better perspective and we are able to assess their significance better. But such a reflection would be possible if we are able to look at things in a detached manner, as if somebody else is examining our project.

We might say, if we empty our mind of its normal content, and look at things with an open and fresh mind, we might be able to have a better understanding of our projects. Objectlessness may be a sound move to properly assess the significance of the object. Thus it is no nonsense to say that one can remain attached to the world but in a detached manner, or be interested in it but with disinterest. It is well known that the aestheticians have often recommended disinterested interest while one enjoys a piece of art. Interest normally refers to some purpose or some sort of utility. An art piece may have a utility for you might fix it somewhere in your drawing room. But to enjoy an art piece you do not think as to what it is going to give you or how it is going to be of some use to you. Thus you do not have any utilitarian interest in the art object. You are disinterested. But you are interested in it. It catches you like a magnet and for a while you are lost. If such a state of mind can be possible in the enjoyment of art, it can also be possible in performing actions.

In *the Mayor of Casterbridge,* Thomas Hardy somewhere remarked that happiness is an occasional episode in a general drama of pain. For most people this may be true. However, the occasional episodes may provide us strength to endure the pains and misery which occupy most of our lives. We have noticed that a good amount of pain or misery is a consequence of our own doings both in the individual and collective contexts. A proper understanding of our place in the existence, our relationships with our fellow beings, and occasional reflection on the nature and possible consequences of our doings might enable us to live a more satisfactory life.

Life and Death.

'Live as if you were to die tomorrow, learn as if you were to live forever.' M.K.Gandhi.

"You cannot live without dying." J. Krishnamurthy

Two major events mark alpha and omega of life – birth and death. There are various views and various contexts in which both these events are viewed – these are biological, personal, social, legal, cultural and religious. Bracketing these, let us view these events from the point of experience - how their awareness occurs in our experience and in what way this awareness moulds our experience if at all. The awareness of these events generally occurs from a distance, that is, in relation to other human beings or in relation to other living beings. We learn about them that they characterize all living beings through our experience. These are events among many other events. There is nothing special about them. If they have to do with individuals who have been related to us or who have been close or distant to us in some way and if matters other than mutual human concerns – such as property etc., are concerned, these events may become significant for us, otherwise they remain as part of the routine or part of life as it goes on. It should be noted that we do not have any experience of either birth or death from first person point of view.

What happens when a human being is born? Two very important considerations have to be borne in mind when we reflect on this question. First what is the gender, secondly what is the social and economic status and condition of the parents? Parents or the family celebrate the birth of the child. Obviously, the celebration of the birth would differ from family to family depending on the status and the condition of the family. Celebrations are also determined by the culture and tradition to which the family belongs. There are unfortunate cases also.. Conceptions or births outside wedlock are sometime treated in an inhuman and undignified way. Births, as everybody knows are treated as legal or illegal, moral or immoral depending on whether they occur within the accepted or unaccepted relationship between the two members of the couple. There are also pressures which lead to attempts to restrict and control births. Thus births are not always welcome.

For some it makes a great difference, if the birth of a son is an occasion of celebration, while the birth of a daughter is considered as misfortune. In some communities people go to the extent as to kill the girl child. In our times, when it has become possible technologically to know about the gender of the child pre-natally, people have the embryo destroyed in its nascent stage if it happens to be of a female. Even if the girls are allowed to live, they are not treated at par with the sons. As compared to the sons they are under-nourished, and not allowed to get educated. There is a change in the situation, but it is slow and not very wide spread.

An expected, awaited and accepted birth of a child not only marks the beginning of a new life of an individual, it also brings about a radical change in the family structure. Again generalizations can not be illuminative, for it would depend on the level and quality of the awareness of other family members including the parents how the birth of the child would affect the family. The number of the children and their gender would also be important variables. This much, perhaps can be said with some certainty that the newly born would divide the attention of the members of the family. It would also affect the budget of the family. There would be a new member to take care of.

Imagine a mother working on the roadside, giving a hug to her newly born or perhaps feeding it, while she has respite for a few moments from her work. The glow on the two faces could be rated amongst the most cherished of human feelings. This was an extreme example. In more normal conditions the scenes would have richer description but the essential feature would remain more or less the same. The birth of a child is a beginning of a saga which may or may not make a radical difference not only to the family but to the whole human existence. It is endowed with immense possibilities. Tagore is supposed to have said that every new born is a new hope for the world.

In our country there is a belief that the birth of a child is a cosmic event. The configuration of the planets at the time and place of the birth of the child determine the temperament, deportment, capabilities, occupation, marriage and children, events of gains or losses, health and sickness, the span of life and death itself. In other words, every child carries a blue-print with itself. Its life unfolds strictly according to this blue print. Added to this belief is another belief which relates to the past life of the child.

It is supposed that the manner in which the child had lived in her or his past life, the kind of actions she or he had performed in that life, that is, the good or bad deeds that she or he has committed in her or his past life, determine first, where and when she or he would take her or his next birth, and in what form. The actions of her or his past life would also determine what she or he is going to get out of her or his present life. These beliefs leave little scope for the individual to act on her or his free will. In order to avoid such a fatal result, another belief is added according to which the individual is actually free to act when it comes to her or his present life. It is true that the deeds of the past life determine the fate in the present life, but the future allows the individual full freedom to act freely and to modify and improve on her or his fate when it comes to the future life.

It is not necessary to discuss the validity of these beliefs. What is to be noted is the fact how the birth of the newly born is accepted and understood in relation to the life to come in different cultures. Obviously, birth means entry of an individual in the world, which has consequences both for the individual as well as the world in which the individual is born. Another individual means an addition to already existing population and consequently a stress on the available resources. The individual is not merely a consumer; s/he might add to or enrich the resources also. A child may be born with a silver spoon in her mouth or may have to face hunger very soon depending on the strata where it is born. Later in life, in the moments of leisure it is likely that having lived through and having reflected on the vicissitudes of life, one may come to realize as to how the human birth and life should be viewed. Such a view may be in terms of having lived a life of

Some people would wish to be born again and again. There may be various reasons underlying such a desire. They may feel that their desires have yet remained unfulfilled or they may feel that they had a mission which did not come to complete fruition and they need still to be there in order to complete it. There are others who declare the world as full of suffering and so not a place worth living. So the best thing is not to be attached to it. Thus the goal should be not to be born again. In other words, the significance of birth is assessed in relation to the quality of life in the world. Besides, there are beliefs which are inherited from generation to generation. These beliefs are related to the nature of life, world and the whole existence. They may be understood as metaphysical beliefs though everyone may not be able to support them with reasons nor may care to do so.

Some of these beliefs are that there is an after life and there has been an earlier life. Most Hindus believe that one passes from one life to another and this process goes on.

Some would like to be able to get out of the chain of lives. In other cultures, it is believed that existence in afterlife has to be there, for the actions and deeds of the life in the world would be judged and fruits or punishment would be awarded according to the quality of those deeds. The belief in the afterlife is accompanied with the belief in other world or worlds. These worlds are also visualized according to the type of deeds of their inhabitants. Hindus believe in several *lokas* (worlds) including *naraka* – hell, and *swarga* – heaven. Others believe that the world in which we live is the only world that there is and there is no other life than the one we live through in this world.

Another very important belief has to do with the moral order maintained in cosmic scheme. The type of life allotted to an individual in after life the type of place an individual is allowed to inhabit after his death, are determined by the type of deeds he had done as we have already noted. No misdeed can pass without proper punishment and similarly no good deed can go unrewarded according to the belief in the cosmic moral order. Unfortunately this does not seem to be an actuality in the world in which we live. Though there may be people who may suffer for their misdeeds and some who may be rewarded for their good deeds, generally it seems as if there is no relationship in what one does and what one enjoys. Thus the belief in the cosmic moral order for some people is merely a make belief or a pious wish.

While most of us remain busy in meeting the immediate needs as they arise out of the necessities of living, some of us also think and reflect if life has a meaning, if there is a purpose for which we exist. The theists would think that there is a purpose that they have to fulfill and that has been divinely ordained, only they have to find it out what it is and live according to it. Some may decide to have an aim or object to guide in their living, even if they may not believe in a divine or unknown cosmic scheme. This consideration leads to a distinction between what may be called a vegetative life and a reflective life. Socrates believed that an unexamined life is not its worth. Some wise men of ancient times advised men to reflect on themselves and their lives. 'Know thyself', has been suggested both in our culture as well as in Greek culture. One may find the equivalent advice in other cultures also.

Living self-consciously may add to our miseries or may enrich our life beyond measure. As, already noted, the greater part of our life remains occupied with immediate concerns. We meet these concerns mostly in a very constricted way without having any regard to other people or the surroundings or the other living beings. Not only horizontally, in temporal sense also our gaze does not go very far from the present. We are not able to visualize the consequences of our action in remote future. Reflection on what we do, what we think, makes us more intensely aware of the inconsistencies, disparities, and conflicts that characterize life all over. This might generate tensions and anxieties. However, reflection if carried on in a proper way may also illumine the ways to counter the anomalies and get rid of the tensions. But what possibly can be the meaning of proper reflection.

Reflecting on oneself, in the first instance, may mean turning away from the external, that is, the given, the objects, the things there. In a sense, let us close our eyes. Unfortunately there is no way to close our ears and other senses. We may abstain for a while from eating or drinking and thus may control our taste sensation, but the same cannot be held about the touch sensation. However, it is also evident that eyes or visual sensation has a dominant role in keeping us busy about the world there. Now, once we are able to turn our gaze on our own self, what do we encounter? Hume, a Scottish philosopher of 18th century, said that he could not find there anything except some feeling of cold or warmth. We may add that we become aware of some thought or some memory, or some sort of desire or perhaps some errand which we may have to fulfill. Our awareness may also involve that we are conscious of something, that is, we may also be aware that we are aware.

Now the thing to be noticed here is that though we have turned ourselves away from the world outside or the world there, we are still occupied with objects of some sort. They are private in the sense that what I entertain at a given moment is not observable from outside, that is, it is not open for inspection to other person. Yet a distinction is there between my being aware of myself and my being aware of something. This distinction falls within my own experience. Suppose I close my eyes then I do not see anything outside. Yet something appears on my mental screen or there are ideas which come to my awareness. So it might be pointed out that I have still not succeeded in completely turning away from the objects of the world. In order to completely turn away from the objects, there should be nothing to keep my consciousness occupied with. I should be in a state in which I am not aware of a thought, a desire, a feeling or a project or a memory or anything whatsoever. Some yogic exercises are precisely oriented in such a direction.

It is a difficult exercise though not an impossible one. Even when I do not consciously try to be in such a state, sometime it so happens as if everything has blacked out and there is nothing for me to keep busy with – a complete empty state. Such a state does not last long though. Such a state of mind is the proper state to launch a self examination. But emptiness offers nothing to be examined. Now, it seems that the examination of life would involve a different kind of self reflection. Perhaps what is meant by self reflection in that context is examining our feelings, desires and projects, and beliefs the experiences that we had and the deeds we performed. What one has to see is whether they are worth having and pursuing. Such an enquiry would presuppose some more general principles or guide lines in the light of which such an enquiry could be carried through.

But do we know as to what these principles or guide lines are? It may be said that we generally act under the guidance of such principles – consciously or unconsciously. But the point is whether there are such clear principles? Are they trans-cultural and universal or they are culture bound? Are they beyond change or keep on changing with times? If more than one, how are they related with each other? Can they be arranged in some kind of hierarchy? These questions and thinking about them is part of what is understood by self reflection. So, on the one hand, one has to examine whether certain ends or projects are worth pursuing, what we think is right and consistent, what we are doing is the right thing to do, what we have done was right or wrong, and on the other hand one has to enquire as to what are the basic or guiding principle which can guide us in our examination.

If such is the understanding of self reflection, it is clear that most of us seldom self reflect. Even if we find an occasion to do so, we do not go very far in our search. Thus to break the routine of day to day business, give a pause and think about ourselves and become aware as to what is going on, becomes a task – a very important task. It is only such a task which lends significance to life. It is such a pause that Albert Camus, an Algerian philosopher of the last century, found significant in the routine to which Sisyphus was bound. (In Greek mythology, the king of Corinth, who was condemned in the Hades – a nether world in afterlife, to push a rock up the hill, which would keep on rolling down all the time.) No doubt there are many other ways to seek the worth of life and naturally that depends on the recognition of certain given values and ideals that are cherished in a certain society at a certain time. Even these values and ideals need to be examined and assessed from time to time. As Nietzsche, a German philosopher, pointed out they need to be re-evaluated.

This can not be gainsaid that if one realizes that the human life has a distinction of its own and has to be distinguished from the living business of all other living beings, then the exercise of self reflection can not be neglected. Human life has often been experienced and described both in negative and positive terms depending on the experiential history of the one who has been living it. The interesting thing is that whether the description is negative or it is positive it seems to have a tenuous connection with what actually happens. To whichever class or position may an individual belong, life offers all kinds of experiences. There may be deprivations and there may be affluence. There may be sufferings and there may be joys. There may be storms and there may be calm. There may be cryings and there may be laughters. The mix in each case will be different from the other. In some cases some one type may dominate, while in the other some other type may be case.

The whole point is how one takes the mix. Each individual has his own way to take the things. It seems suffering in one form or the other is ubiquitous. The degree, intensity, frequency and quantum of suffering may be different in one case than the other. One may think of Buddhism in which the existence in the world itself has been characterized as full of sorrow. One more thing should be borne in mind and that is what may be suffering for one may not be so for the other. One may enjoy all the risks and pains involved in mountaineering while for some others these risks or pains may be discouraging. But there are some sufferings which may be accepted as sufferings universally, for example, poverty, hunger, lack of shelter, disease, and the infirmities of old age or bereavement.

For some these or other sufferings are like punishment. Often it is said that one suffers for what one has done, if not in this life then in the past life. For some others they are not punishment but kind of tests which one has to undergo in order attain or realize the better part of the self or gain wisdom. Still others may treat them as part of the mix which is life and for whom it is folly to expect from life all pleasure and no pain. Some treat them as proper consequences of misdeeds. Where it is not possible to find their source in some misdeeds, and appear to be undeserved, it is either taken to be owing to some divine or cosmic purpose which remains hidden from the knowledge of the mortals, or is treated as a conundrum of divine justice. Still others trace it to man-made organization which is full of inconsistencies and disparities and which needs to be changed. Thus life as full of sufferings has led people to ask as to why suffering is there and also to ways to put up with the fact of suffering in life.

When we do not know how to account for whatever happens to us while we live, we look for other ways to understand life. Some would think it to be futile to ask for any meaning in life or make sense of it, for the simple reason that there is no meaning in life. It is better to live rather than waste life in looking for the meaning of life. Some take life to be absurd or as a joke. Life is also treated like a play or drama which amuses someone up there. Life has also been taken as a gift. One should be grateful for it and should be careful to live it well. Since it is given once, one has to make the best of it.

It appears that if life is looked at only from the point of the one who lives it, that is from the point of view as to what one can gain from it, or how one can derive pleasure out of it, then it would offer one kind of picture. If it is looked at from the point of the totality within which the individual finds herself or himself, and if one treats it as an opportunity to do one's mite for the good or betterment of this totality, life would be full of opportunities and challenges. This later view is also likely to form or modify one's outlook to all the hazards, tensions and sufferings that one is likely to meet while trying to actualize the potentialities and meeting the challenges. The wisdom of great wise people of the world supports this later approach to life.

Thus the quest for the meaning of life, or the purpose of life, is not confined wholly to the individual herself or himself alone, and the necessity for self-reflection, seem to be crucial for living life and getting the best out of it.

One does not live indefinitely or for a very long period. One is born, grows, decays and dies. This seems to be the fate of any living being, including humans. Life comes to a close, though there is a tendency to keep the idea of the terminus at bay as long as one can. Unless one is not terminally sick, or not under some dire and calamitous situation, one hardly ever thinks or bothers about death. It is funny that while we see people being killed, murdered or dying natural deaths, the thought of death does not bother us much. In a way it is a boon. To keep on thinking of death and postponing the business of living would be foolish, absurd and painful. However, the awareness that at some point of time the life would cease to be has an important role for the business of living itself.

Let us for a while think about amassing wealth and property without limit. There may be many reasons for doing so. One always feels the need of money to fulfill so many necessities and desires. Possession of property and assets also creates a feeling of security and confidence. May be one thinks to leave sufficient support for one's children when one is not there. Apart from all these considerations, amassing wealth has a toxic effect. One does it just because one is driven to do so. Unfortunately in the event of death, the amassed wealth has no meaning for the dead. One had to spend one's life making all kind of compromises with principles, one had to be indifferent and cruel to others, one had to lie and conspire, and what not, though one may have had pleasures and must have enjoyed oneself too. Yet death nullifies the life the individual lived. This story and reactions to it have been repeated *ad nauseum*. Yet it has made no dent.

Normally we live mostly unreflectively and death, of course, gives us no opportunity to reflect, yet people sometime think about death and develop beliefs and attitudes towards it. Basically, there are two approaches. According to one approach, death is not an end of life altogether. It marks the termination of one life and not of all life. There is life after death. Such a life has been conceived in different ways in different cultures or ways of thinking. So far as Indian thinking is concerned, what kind of life one would have after death would depend on what kind of deeds one has performed in this life. The kind of sufferings or comforts one is able to enjoy in this life, according to Indian vision, is determined by what one had done in one's past life. Thus the chain of lives one has to live through the various births is completely determined by the quality of deeds one performs. This is supposed to be determined by the cosmic moral order.

In Semitic religions such as Judaism, Christianity and Islam, too, the fruits one is likely to have in the after-existence are determined by the type of deeds one has performed in this birth. There is no mention of life before the present life. Also, in Islam it is supposed that those who die would remain in their graves and would suffer hell or peace as the case may be before they are resurrected and face the Judge on the day of judgement. The important thing to notice is that the afterlife of whatever sort is finally determined for its quality by the deeds one has performed on this earth in the present life.

There has been another way to conceive the continuity of life chain in which death merely serves as a pause. The famous Urdu poet Ghalib wonders in one of his famous couplet what happens to those who die and disappear from the earth. He speculates that some of them re-appear in the forms of some beautiful flowers. In similar vein Edvard Munch, the famous painter, wrote, "From my rotting body, flowers shall grow and I am in them and that is eternity." In fact, the belief is that after the death, when the body is finally dispensed with, it mingles with the five elements. It is well known that all that exists on the earth is ultimately reducible to, at least in frame of thought, the five elements. The atoms of these elements are considered to be eternal while their appearances in various configurations and forms are supposed to be transitory. Thus the chain of life continues for eternity. In such a view no hell or heaven are imagined to exist besides this earth. There are neither apprehensions nor expectations of any kind which one may experience in respect of a supposed future life.

There is yet another way in which the afterlife is imagined. In this view death is suppose to emancipate us from the uncertain kind of existence that one has to live through on this earth which is a mix of all kinds of happenings bringing with them, sometime miseries and sometime pleasure and fortune. Socrates, while going to sip hemlock, imagines that he may be able to meet the great wise men of past and it would be such a nice experience that he is likely to have in the other world. Helen Keller imagined that it would be possible for her to see in the other world. In India many believe that after death miseries and sufferings that one has to undergo in this world would be no more there and one would be able to enjoy a life of happiness and peace. In fact, in one set of the beliefs, it is supposed that if one disciplines oneself and lives a life of virtue, one is likely to move in a state of being after death in which the chain of lives would cease altogether. This is supposed to be highest kind of state one could hope for.

It is interesting to note that while an eternal state of happiness and peace is supposed to be the highest state, it has not been understood or visualized as to what kind of experience it would be. Nevertheless it has been claimed that such a state is attainable, provided one had gone through certain recommended disciplinary procedure.

In the above brief sketch, we have been through the various views and approaches as determined by individual, social, cultural, and religious contexts, in respect of life and death. We have not said anything about the very important emotions of love and hate, and the relationship between man and woman, which occupy a substantial part of life experience. Reader would find these aspects treated in two separate essays included in this text. It would be noticed that the writer's inclination tilts towards a life of action directed by reflection as grounded in a wider horizon beyond merely immediate survival needs. In such a perspective death would constitute a summation of a meaningful story.

Finite or Infinite

"The man is not complete; he is yet to be."

"That we cannot absolutely possess the infinite being is not a mere intellectual proposition. It has to be experienced and this experience is bliss."
Rabindranath Tagore.

Whatever comes into being, remains in existence for a while and then comes to an end or disappears from the existence. This saying prevails from ancient times and has never been assailed. From this it follows that every existent being is mortal and finite. It may be pointed out that this is true only in respect of the beings which are not ultimate. It is also believed that there are certain ultimate beings or substances which have always been there and would continue to remain there. Their forms may undergo changes but they themselves stay as they always have been. Such a view has been acceptable both to the metaphysicians and the scientists in different ways. Metaphysicians talk about substance and its attributes, while scientists talk about ultimate bits and their compound compositions. What exactly is the nature of these ultimate beings or being may remain a subject for constant investigation.

Thus there are beings that perish and there are beings or being which persist. This duality is sometime taken to be inherent in all things or beings and sometime has remained confined to two distinct kinds of entities. Ontology, the science of being, demands explanation of ultimate beings on the one hand and the beings which come into existence then perish on the other. Sometimes the perishable beings are considered as perishable forms of some being which remains imperishable. The idea is that if there is something it must have always been there, though it may not have been there in the same form always. There can be nothing which can be generated out of nothing. So if there is a being it must have been preceded by some other being which could not have been radically different from it and so must have been the same being though in a different form.

In Indian ontology there have been other views in relation to this issue. According to one view what appears to be as a pluralistic and changing phenomena is deceptive because it is not real. In contrast, only that which is not subject to change, which has always been, is and will be, and which is also the only being is the only reality. Such a reality is transcendent. The other view takes both the change and plurality as real and consequently also accepts the fact of things coming into existence and perishing after a while. It is not necessary to believe that they are associated or connected with something ultimate in any possible way. In yet another view, it is the imperishable that appears in the perishables. In the *Taitirya Upanisad,* we are told that in the beginning, the Absolute desired to become many – *bahu syam,* and then having undergone *tapas,* the Absolute created all this – *idam sarvam asrajata,* and then entered into it – *anupravisat* (2, 6).

However, when we concentrate on human existence, no one denies the phenomenon of birth, life and death, for they are so patent. These facts of human existence embed it in a spatio-temporal frame. A human being is born at some place and at some time. Having lived for a period, the human being dies at some place and at some time. Thus a human being does not live for ever and is not immortal. That human beings wish for immortality, some even believe in it and would want to attain it, are well known facts. In spite of such a wish, immortality has not been attained by any human being so far.

Though one wishes to be immortal, yet the fact of mortality and finitude is pressed on one's consciousness in several ways. The fact that it is not within one's willing where one would take one's birth, the fact that one has to depend completely for some time on others for survival, the fact that one needs the help and support of other human beings later in life in several ways, the fact that one has to do something in order to earn one's bread, the fact that one can do or perform only that which one's body and intellect can support, all these point to various kinds of dependence, a human being has to suffer. These facts show that a human being has various kinds of limitations which describe the various dimension of one's finitude.

It may be said, that though a human being has several limitations, one is not completely determined in one's actions. A human being is also said to be free to choose, to decide, to act freely and for this reason it is possible to hold her or him responsible for what she or he does. Some go to the extent as to say that there is no action in which a human being is not free. Sartre, a well known French philosopher said man is condemned to be free. That a human being can do whatever one desires or wishes, has both been argued for and contested. The simple point is that if it were possible for a human being to attain whatever one desired, there would have been no problem and everyone would have been happy. This is not so. On the contrary it has also been noted that in spite of all possible efforts, one often fails to get what is one's due. The issue remains debatable because the complexity involved in the dynamics of an action remains unattended.

First thing to note is that no action can be performed, unless some conditions are fulfilled. The most important of these conditions are the bodily capacity, acquired skill, and relevant know-how. If the body is immature, if it is sick or maimed, or one does not know how to move one's limbs, and one does not know how and in what direction to move, obviously, the action cannot be get done. One of the major contributions of science has been to make us aware of the forces which make our movements possible. Most of us are hardly aware of the fact that if the force of gravity which if were not operative it would not have been possible for us to make simple movements of walking or grasping. What we take to be voluntary physical movements are made possible by the natural forces. The full realization of this fact dawned when entry into outer space and experiments in space could become possible. Even now, in spite of the knowledge of this fact the major portion of humanity is unaware of this fact. There are other similar features of nature which permit us several types of enabilities and of which we are as much aware as we are of the force of gravity, for example, the presence of oxygen in the atmosphere. It is only when the atmosphere is polluted to an unbearable degree or we find ourselves at very high altitudes that we become aware of the difficulty in breathing and thereby of the significance of oxygen.

Recent advances in bio-chemistry, neurology and bio-technology indicate that the physical aspect of the personality is largely determined by the genes. It was already known that the emotional temperament is a function of glandular secretions. The question relating to heredity versus environment has always remained a live issue.

Apart from nature, there are certain other aspects which enable us to think and act as we do and in the ignorance of these aspects we think that we do them because of our own initiative and free will. We hardly ever realize that the language because of which we are able to express our vital needs is available to us because we are born into a linguistic community. Words come to our help just as oxygen enables us to breath. Even the bodily gestures indicating our needs and feelings come to us because of our unconscious learning from the social surroundings. The point of all these considerations is that most of our activities whether they have to do with our thinking or our actions are possible because of features on which we do not have any control. Our dependence on them shows our limitations and our finitude. Since we are hardly aware of them, we do not realize that we should be grateful to them. We should recognize their support and be conscious of our size.

Not merely language but even the ways in which we think, the kind of beliefs we have, the sort of things we like or dislike, the things that we revere or hate, are greatly determined by the culture to which we belong. Most of these beliefs, tendencies and attitudes which we have adopted from our culture become part of our psychic background without our being conscious of them. It is only in times of crisis that we become conscious of them and become reflective about them. So far as the individuals who have had the fortune of having been through the educational institutions are concerned, most of them move with their academic baggage. All these factors show that what is supposed to be free choice or decision is after all not that free. It is also true, that without there being a background provided by our previous learning —may be conscious or unconscious, formal or informal, we cannot even think what to say of making a choice or decision. This requires us to be more cautious when we use the term freedom or free will.

This description may be dubbed as some kind of reductionism and just for that reason as an inadequate explanation or understanding of human personality. Those who take this view, claim that it is wrong to reduce the human personality to biochemic, genetic, or socio-cultural factors only. While such a thing may be true in respect of the physical aspect of human personality, it neglects the higher functions which characterize human personality such as intellect, reason, conscience, and imagination, that is, mind. There are others who would add to the list, soul, spirit or self.

Let's pause for a while and understand as to what is understood by mind or soul or spirit. Sometime they are applied as interchangeable terms. One important way in which they are characterized is that they are radically different from the body. What is mind or soul is not body. It is also believed that mind is something separable from the body. It even survives body. In Indian thinking, mind is sometime considered as belonging to body and different from spirit or *atma*. Even though mind is supposed to belong to the body and as different from atma, it is taken to be as that part which survives the death of the body/ in that sense it is called as *suksma sarira*. These ideas are different from those held in Western thinking.

In West, mind is considered to be something not physical. Aristotle believed that Reason (that is mind) is separable from the body. In the Western tradition, mind, reason and consciousness, even soul or spirit are often used in a synonymous way. They are supposed to comprehend all the mental functions, such as thinking, reasoning, imagining, willing, and feeling and so on. Mind is considered to be radically different from body. It has been considered as a different kind of substance. The word substance refers to an entity that endures and is ultimate in some sense. For this reason, soul is also considered as immortal.

There has been a debate about the relationship of mind and body. There is a school of thought according to which nothing can be said with definiteness about mind or consciousness. It is better to ignore it altogether for it is not tangible, cannot be observed and hence the concept of mind explains nothing. In order to understand human personality, one must concentrate on behaviour, on physical movements and changes in the body, the anatomy and physiology of brain and nervous system. These are amenable to observation, their movements can be measured. They can be located and identified and their functions can be understood. There are others who think that this approach is inadequate for it leaves the experiential aspect unexplained. To understand subjective aspect of experience it is necessary to understand consciousness. From the Indian point of view, the subjective consciousness underlies all mental phenomena and experience in its various modes. Since it underlies, supports, makes experience possible, it cannot itself be made an object of experience. That is why it cannot be approached and understood in the same way as one can understand any given object or phenomenon.

Still others would like to understand experiential aspects as functions of brain and the neurons. In the present context it is not necessary to look for the conclusive views about the debate, first because final conclusions are not available, secondly the context of the present discussion does not require us to go into this debate further. For our present purposes the important point is that there is an aspect of the personality which is considered to be as different from its physical aspects and which is supposed to be independent of them and which is also considered to be ever enduring as compared to the body. It is body or the physical aspect which is subject to mortality. So far as the mental or spiritual aspect is concerned, it is not perishable. It is difficult to say what happens to it when a human being dies, yet there is a strong belief that it is only the body that becomes lifeless not the mind.

From the earliest times, a belief that there is a man inside the man, whose movements are not obstructed by any physical barrier, who can move freely anywhere, has persisted in various forms. Sometimes, the phenomenon of dream is supposed to support a belief of this kind. Though this belief may not be accepted just in this form, its presence is widely accepted in the form of the freedom of thought. It is often said that one can enchain or imprison the body but one can not imprison the mind or soul. The freedom of thought seems to be inalienable. But what is thinking any way? One can think of any thing one likes. Anything can be an object of thought. However, thinking is not merely calling to presence of an object. It should also be clear that calling to presence is not like having something presented to someone actually like the performance of some Alladin's lamp. Calling to presence to consciousness, merely means that having some object there before the consciousness.

However, thinking would not stop once there is an object present to a consciousness. Thinking allows consciousness to move from one object to another. It facilitates movement from one object to another object or from characteristic of an object to its other characteristic. Since an object is placed in a network of objects, it can be viewed from any number of angles exhibiting its infinite aspects. Thus thinking has the possibility to keep on moving for ever. As is the general experience of any body, thinking comes to be terminated because of the stringency of action. One cannot remain in the thinking mood for ever, for one has to fulfill various other needs, and that necessitates, decision and action.

But thinking is not merely a movement from one object to the other. The relationships between the objects are discovered in various ways. Either the relationship points to some kind of association between the objects which may be purely accidental or it may be so close that the thought of one object necessarily brings to notice the thought of the other object. In between there may be various kinds of relationships according to how close a thought is to another thought. Thought does not stop here. It further reflects on the place of an object or its characteristic amongst the others, that is, what place does an object or its characteristic occupy in relation to others of its kind. When placing an object in this manner various qualifiers become relevant – higher or lower, important or trivial, worthy or unworthy, good or bad, right or wrong, true or false, valuable or valueless, and so on.

The use of such qualifiers suggests that there must be some basis which allows thinking to move in a certain way. This may relate to the place something occupies in the life of the individual or may have to do with the quality of relationships within which she is placed (family or society or the world). What positive contribution a thing makes to life or existence or in what way a thing would affect adversely life or existence would determine where it would be placed in the totality of objects. At the moment we are concerned with the non-physical aspect of human personality. Thinking is one such and an essential aspect which is said to be determined by its own laws and is not subject to kind of laws of nature as body is. This self-determination is its freedom. But even such a self-determined activity functions within certain conditions. Thinking which moves through concepts has to live through language. Thinking has a dual relationship with language. It precedes language. It moves through language. Language makes it possible and it sometime enriches language.

Now language as given, determines thinking by the culture to which the language belongs. As is evident language is a product of the collective activity of an entire people over an indefinitely long period. It's a living activity in the sense that it is maintained and sustained by the actual speech and writing of a people. A word is a career of meanings which it is endowed with the usages actually carried through by a community of speakers. These usages are indicative of the ways of living which involve action and reaction with the world around. Naturally anyone thinking and using language is engaged in an activity comparable to the life of a drop in a river. Though, mostly we are not aware of this background. Thus the freedom of thought has to be viewed in a restricted manner.

Thinking can also be viewed as a reflective function which helps the individual in assessing and evaluating whatever s/he accosts or whatever happens to her or him. If this function operates unhindered by narrow self interests and passions it becomes an illuminating orientation and can serve as a guide in difficult situations.

Now while we talk of the non-physical, rational or immortal being indwelling the body, we may or may not have in our mind the idea of self-reflective illuminating activity of the mind. The question whether the non-physical part of the human personality is actually independent of the body, whether it survives the death of the body, would remain debatable in spite of the fact that a very large number of people all over the world tend to believe in the immortality of soul. However, the experience seems to confirm the presence of the self-reflective feature in the make up of human personality, though it is not always active.

The strangeness of the other, or a suspicion in the motivation of the other, the difficulty or impossibility of fulfillment of certain desires, the feeling of insecurity as a consequence of scarcity of resources, desire to attain more power, pelf, and control over others are some of the factors which interfere in the proper performance of self-reflective activity They do not merely interfere, they also brush it aside or rather give it a wrong direction. This constant constriction within oneself to the utter neglect of the right of the other to live decently accompanied by the feeling of insecurity and misapprehension is indicative of the finitude of the human existence. It can also be seen as a source of ills which generally afflict mankind.

It is to be noted that human existence like the existence of all other beings or things is essentially finite for the beings come into existence and go out of it. None of them have any control on the features of appearance and disappearance. Yet the excellence of human existence has often been gauged by one's courage to live – to live positively. Facing the various hurdles and be through the struggles which life offers with vision and patience, with love and concern, with magnanimity and surrender neutralizes human finitude. The possibility that individuals can overcome their narrowness or in other words, that they can overcome themselves may indicate that they have something common with the infinite. But assuming oneself to be infinite or immortal would be to relapse back in the worst delusion with which a finite being can suffer

Yet, normally we tend to be oblivious of death, even in spite of the fact that we do notice and sometime we have to notice people dying. Somehow it does not occur to me that some day I am also going to meet the same fate. There are, of course, occasion when the awareness of coming death may take the form of intense and disturbing feeling. In old age, being sick for a long time, or being a terminal patient the feeling of death becomes gnawing. It gets more intensified, if my near or dear ones still need care and support. Death of other people, though sometime traumatic for oneself in case the person who is dead has been close to us, does not normally disturb us.

These are facts of our day to day living. But people have desired immortality. They have wished that death may never come to them. Like light, wisdom, truth and goodness, immortality has also been aimed at as a goal worthy of achievement. This has also been a part of beliefs, that no one can survive death with body. There have been some exceptions to this belief as narrated in some stories as narrated in the *puranas*. Thus immortality had come to be associated with the non-physical part of human personality. In fact, it would be wrong to call it a 'part' for it has been accepted as an integral entity in itself. As *atma* it is said to be an entity which can neither be burnt, nor be dried, nor be destroyed as *Gita* teaches us. In other words, normal natural laws do not apply to it. Thus attaining immortality means attaining the realization of one's real nature. To realize that one is atma, one is not body, is to realize that one is not perishable.

While the notion of *moksa* as a *purusartha* in the Indian thinking has been seen as emancipation from the physical, and as merging of atma or consciousness with the ultimate being or cosmic consciousness, the desire for immortality has another dimension which seems to have been considered as a source of all ills. According to paurnic tradition, there have been *devas, gandharvas,* and *rakshas* (also called, *asuras, daityas* or *danavas*) besides *manavas*. Since devas had the privilege of having drunk the nectar, they became immortal and they also had a privileged habitat called *'swarga'* (or paradise). *Rakshas* were not allowed to have the nectar and they live in the lower or netherland. However, the leaders in the *rakshas* have always tried to attain immortality. For this they have undergone all kind of penances and have performed *tapas* for long time. As a result they have succeeded in inviting the Supreme God (in most cases, Siva) and getting boons.

As is well known, they have always wished for immortality and have sought boons intending to save them from impending danger of death. The boons have been generally ambiguous. They apparently seemed to ward of the danger of death so far as the understanding of the raksas was concerned. But it also meant that the manner of death would be unusual and may take place at some appropriate occasion. The stories of Hiranayakasyapa, Ravana, Kansa, and many others illustrate these very features.

These stories also point to the delusive nature of the feeling of immortality. Each of the *raksasas* who was blessed with a boon and who thought that now there is no way that he could be killed or that there is no one who could kill him, therefore, he is going to live forever, became so proud and vain that instead of doing any good to people, he started humiliating, torturing and killing people in all possible ways. The being of a rakshas thus became a source of cosmic calamity like any other natural source of calamity. In fact these devilish personalities became so powerful, that ultimately the Supreme God Himself had to descend in the form of a human being and had to overcome and kill these devilish beings. This reminds one of the famous comment of Krisna in *Gita*, that He had to descend whenever the sin became rampant on earth and had to punish the culprit and thus save and protect the virtuous people. It is interesting to note that the evil personality needed a God in human form to destroy it.

Thus the teaching of descent of God in the form of human being and destroying the evil force can be seen as a lesson to guard against the desire of immortality. Possibility of victory over death seems to be closely connected with the vain pride being a possible source of all that is cruel and violent. In the coming times it would again become pressing to be occupied with the thought of death and immortality. As is well known the advances in bio-technology are sometime seen as moving towards a stage when it would be possible to delay death as long as possible. It is also obvious that such a thing would normally be beyond the means and capacity of the ordinary citizen. The result can be visualized in the form of coming together of all those features which have characterized the life of devilish personality. The classical story of Bhasmasura, as told in the ancient times, should be treated as a warning against the possible dangers of the advances in bio-technology.

Bhasmasura was supposed to be a demon that performed penances to please God Shiva in order to gain a boon in order to put on fire whatever he would put his hand on. Once the boon was granted he was tempted to see the boon was really effective. The devil first chose Shiva himself as his subject. It was Visnu who saved Shiva from the trouble by assuming the form of a beautiful dancer and in the course of the dance Visnu put his hand on his own head. Bhasmasura became enamoured of the dancer and started to dance in the same way and put his hand on his head just as Visnu had done. And thus destroyed himself. The moral of the story is that devilish power is suicidal.

It appears that the wish for immortality is neither likely to be fulfilled nor it is desirable to have it fulfilled. The fact that human beings are mortal and finite beings, in the sense that they have a limited span of life and there are limits to their capacities and abilities seems to be irrefutable. While this is true that human beings have limits to their capacities and abilities, yet it has not been possible to gauge these limits in an exact way. History of mankind is documented by episodes of exceptional performances and achievements of certain exceptional individuals. Though the percentage of such individuals is not very large, but the sheer fact that some individuals were able to prove themselves as exceptional, shows that exact scores cannot be fixed.

Besides, each individual has in her or his make up inbuilt a mechanism which allows her or him to take account of her or his thoughts, action and behaviour. Though it is not actualized in each individual in the same way and the same degree, yet it can be seen as craving to transcend the present. In what directions such transcendence takes place, and in what degree does it succeed, differs from individual to individual. In this transformative process an overcoming of one's finitude can be seen as a constant process. Perhaps it is this tendency or the urge towards going beyond the limit which defines the worth and meaning of human existence.